Visionary Leadership
in Volunteer Programs

Insight and Inspiration from the Speeches of Marlene Wilson

Acknowledgments

I want to thank all those colleagues in volunteer administration who have given so much to this profession. Special thanks to Jane Leighty Justis and Betty Stallings who gave me the idea for this book and kept nagging me until it was done.

I am most grateful to two wonderful young women, my daughter, Lisa, and my assistant, Nancy Giehl, for being careful and honest readers and editors and much needed cheerleaders. A special thank you to my talented son, Rich, who took the cover photo in Hawaii on my 75th birthday. Also, I am extremely thankful for the superb editing and publishing skills of Susan Ellis and Cara Thenot.

Visionary Leadership in Volunteer Programs: Insight and Inspiration from the Speeches of Marlene Wilson. Copyright © 2008 by Marlene Wilson. All rights reserved. No part of this book may be reproduced in any form, or by electronic or mechanical means, including information storage and retrieval systems without permission in writing from the publisher.

Published by Energize, Inc.
5450 Wissahickon Ave., Ste. C-13
Philadelphia, PA 19144
http://www.energizeinc.com
(215) 438-8342

First Edition
paperback ISBN: 978-0-940576-57-5
e-book ISBN: 978-0-940576-58-2

Library of Congress Control Number: 2008928599

PRINTED IN THE UNITED STATES OF AMERICA

Contents

Reflections on a Friend and Mentor

Betty Stallings and Jane Leighty Justis

Several years ago Marlene and the two of us were sitting together in Marlene's Boulder, Colorado home discussing challenges and opportunities in our lives and careers. This led to a sharing of the phenomenal impact that Marlene had on our personal and professional lives and on the lives of countless others involved in the leadership of volunteer programs. Rather spontaneously and enthusiastically, we began to encourage Marlene to share the legacy of her immensely popular keynote talks in a new book.

What a gift those words were when she delivered them. What a treasure they will be for those of us impacted and inspired by them, as well as for today's and tomorrow's leaders in the evolving profession of leader of volunteer programs.

We were delighted when Marlene responded positively to our impassioned request. In this book she has shared her most popular talks; ones that inspired, challenged and mentored decades of people devoted to volunteerism and the effective leadership of those endeavors. The messages are timeless in their value and, perhaps, are needed more now as we struggle to define and build support for the profession.

Our lives continue to be inspired by the messages in this book, and we are certain that you will read and reread them to gain insights and inspiration for both your personal and professional lives. We profoundly thank Marlene for taking the time to imprint them permanently on our lives and to Energize, Inc. for publishing them.

Personal Reflections by Betty

In the mid 1970s I was in the midst of establishing a volunteer center and had the good fortune of attending a Marlene Wilson seminar in San Francisco. (Our organization could not afford the $10 registration fee, so I volunteered to help at the session!) In the audience of hundreds of people that day, I felt as if Marlene was talking to me. All of my questions, concerns and issues relating to the leadership of volunteers were addressed with humor, insight, practicality, warmth and inspiration. From that moment until the present day, Marlene has been a significant professional and life mentor to me. Marlene's written and spoken messages and metaphors were important messages in guiding my work to develop a creative volunteer center and a touchstone for my later work as a trainer.

Marlene was a tireless pioneer in creating the foundation of the profession of volunteer management. In presenting upwards to 200 talks a year, she shared her vision and wisdom on such topics as creativity, influence, marketing, leadership, time management, burnout, organizational climate, motivation, change, problem solving as well as all of the management and leadership skills needed to effectively lead volunteer programs. Many people speak and write on these topics but Marlene had a unique and refreshing perspective. She was the first one to take an interdisciplinary approach to volunteer management, including basic principles of psychology, communications and business administration. Her talks arose from her passion, experience and infectious optimism. Unlike most talks, hers did not fade over time but rather increased their impact on the listener. People who heard Marlene speak 25 years ago continue to surface stories and enduring lessons learned from those sessions.

As I began to follow in her professional footsteps, I attempted to discover why her talks were so meaningful. For me, several key reasons surfaced.

- She's an amazing storyteller.
- She shares the perfect quotes to illustrate her points.
- Her style of communication gives the impression that she speaks to you personally.
- She shares gentle reassurance and support to the grave challenges facing the profession.
- She engages the audience with questions that prompt each person to tailor the information into practical use for his/her situation.
- At the heart of her messages are the *why* questions, always associated with a practical framework to determine the *how* that would be best to use to resolve issues or challenges personal to the participant.

I might have stayed on as the executive director of the volunteer center if Marlene had not invited me to consider sharing my experience, insights and knowledge with others. With her encouragement (and gentle nudging!) I resigned my position at the volunteer center and launched a new career of training, speaking and writing in the field of volunteerism. I am just one of many fortunate trainers who have been nurtured and mentored by this incredible woman.

When you read the list of Marlene's contributions, accomplishments and recognition in the field, it is astounding, but as someone who has been privileged to become a close colleague and friend, I have witnessed her genuine passion about the field and the personal impact she has had on so many thousands of people who have taken on the position of manager of volunteer resources during the past 30 years.

Personal Reflections by Jane

Like most of my colleagues, many of whom I've known now for over 30 years, I backed into the field of volunteerism. In fact, you couldn't really call it a field. We were a ragtag army of folks who had taken—or been handed —the responsibility of "taking care of those volunteers" in many different kinds of settings.

I was "roped into" agreeing to put on a walkathon in our community. How hard could it be, I asked myself? I would just get my friends to help and we would raise lots of money for this worthy organization. Well, I did—and we did. And, it was one of the most rewarding, but also one of the hardest experiences of my life. I learned that empowering volunteers is both an art and a science. It doesn't just happen. As often is true, when you are successful as a volunteer you get a reward: You get to do it again— only more and bigger and longer! I was asked by the organization to recruit a new volunteer director in my hometown in addition to starting and supervising walkathons in a few other Colorado cities as well. I was terrified!

I knew that if I were to attempt this task, I needed help! I remember having dinner with a friend in Denver soon after I had accepted this challenge. In a serendipitous happening, she told me she had recently heard about a book on volunteer management, and wasn't I doing something with volunteers now?

That was my introduction to Marlene. As I read the wonderful book, *The Effective Management of Volunteer Programs*, I was hooked by her gift for weaving together the heart and the art and the science of management, and applying it to the recruiting and empowering of volunteers. It remains a classic today. My passion for the potential and power of volunteer action was born as I read her book, and it has grown and deepened over the years.

Some are gifted writers, and others are more effective as speakers. Marlene is one of those rare people whose concepts, stories, examples and metaphors are as powerful in print as they are when she speaks about them. As a newcomer to volunteer management, I soaked up all Marlene had to offer like a sponge—reading her books and being in the audience at her workshops and keynote speeches.

Over the past 30 years, I have had an opportunity to hear most all of the speeches contained in this compilation. As I have read them again—years after first hearing them, I remain convinced of the timelessness of her messages.

They are not just about volunteer management skills, but about shaping our lives and defining our passions and choices and values. You will find yourself recalling images and musing about some of her questions long after you have finished her book. You may even come to reexamine, reflect on and possibly reframe some of your basic paradigms about your career and your life. She will "get under your skin"!

One of her greatest gifts to so many of us in the field was the creation of the Volunteer Management Certificate program through the University of Colorado. Within a few years, it was known as the place to come for a great education, but also to have your soul fed and your passion rekindled. Hundreds of people over the years spoke of how their participation in this program had been a life-changing experience. Betty and I were fortunate to serve on Marlene's faculty during those 25 years.

In the 1990s, after many years as a practitioner and trainer in the field of volunteerism, I expanded my passion to include empowering people in the giving of their "treasure" as well as their time and talent. I am the executive director of a family foundation that has as one of its focus areas the promotion of philanthropy and volunteerism. I spend much of my time now working with other funders who also realize that volunteerism — or civic engagement, or citizen participation or whatever term we use — is not just a hobby or a helpful activity, but the bedrock on which this great experiment of democracy is built.

We who share this vision and are passionate about making a difference in this hurting world need Marlene's book. We need to hear her words challenging us and convicting us, as well as encouraging us, laughing with us, and inspiring us.

Left to Right: Jane Leighty Justis, Marlene, and Betty Stallings

We are thrilled that those of us who were personally touched by Marlene's talks will now have this treasured compilation of her finest speeches. But perhaps even more, we are delighted that many who have more recently entered the field can benefit and be inspired by this woman whose contributions to our profession are immeasurable.

We simply cannot imagine the field without Marlene's pioneering leadership to it. From all of us who have stood on her shoulders in our attempt to further the field of volunteerism and to those who will be inspired anew or discover Marlene for the first time by reading her words, we extend an enduring and heartfelt appreciation.

Thank you, Marlene, for this remarkable book. We cannot repay you for the gifts you offer us in these pages, but we can each find our own ways to pass them on.

Betty Stallings, Pleasanton, CA
Jane Leighty Justis, Colorado Springs, CO
Spring 2008

The Life and Times of Marlene Wilson

Her Education

1953: Concordia College, Moorhead, Minnesota. Academic background includes psychology, organizational behavior, and personnel management.

Her Early Jobs

Human resources management for six years at Holly Manufacturing Company, Pasadena, California and Electro Optical Systems (a division of Xerox Corporation).

Her Volunteer Management Career

1968: Helps to create and becomes the first executive director of The Volunteer and Information Center of Boulder County, Colorado. This was the first volunteer center in Colorado and one of only a few existing in the United States. The center became a national model for developing volunteer centers across the country.

1972: Begins traveling beyond Colorado to do training in volunteer management. Since then, over 250,000 people from volunteer organizations and churches have attended her workshops in the United States, Canada and Europe.

Founds the University of Colorado Volunteer Management Certificate Program – the first of its kind to provide volunteer management training for volunteer professionals. Serves as faculty director until the program's end on its 25th anniversary in 1997.

1975: Founds and still serves as president of the publishing and consulting firm, Volunteer Management Associates.

1976: Is editor-in-chief of the journal, *Volunteer Administration* (until 1978).

2001: Hosts the radio talk show, *Ask the Experts*, on KPNX in Phoenix, Arizona.

2003: Serves as advisor to Group Publishing's Church Volunteer Central (until 2005).

2008: Continues to write and consult on a limited basis.

Her Community Volunteer Work

Marlene has served on several boards including:

- The National Board and Executive Committee of Aid Association for Lutherans
- National Board for the Division of Ministry of the Evangelical Lutheran Church of America
- Denver Regional Council of Government
- Boulder Community Hospital
- Church of Joy Leadership Center

Her Publications

1976: *The Effective Management of Volunteer Programs*, only the second title in the volunteer field. It becomes the best-selling work in the field, with over 150,000 copies sold.

1981: Writes *Survival Skills for Managers*.

1983: *How to Mobilize Church Volunteers*, the first work to apply volunteer management principles to the special needs of churches.

1990: *You Can Make a Difference!: Helping Others and Yourself Through Volunteering*, receives the prestigious Benjamin Franklin Award for Best Self-Help Book.

2004: Authors three books in Group Publishing's Volunteer Leadership Series, *Creating a Volunteer-Friendly Church Culture*, *Volunteer Job Descriptions and Action Plans*, and *Volunteer Encouragement, Evaluation and Accountability*. Also, serves as general editor for the six-volume series published in January 2004.

In addition to her books, Marlene has produced a library of workshops on both audiotape and videotape, to help volunteer organizations and churches everywhere learn from her ideas and expertise.

Her Recognition

1982: Distinguished Member Award from the Association for Volunteer Administration

1989: Honorary Doctor of Divinity degree from Wartburg Seminary

1989: Outstanding Alumni Award from Concordia College, Moorhead, Minnesota

1999: National Volunteer Leader Award from the American Hospital Association

2002: Lifetime Member Award by the Association for Volunteer Administration in recognition of her life-long contributions to the field of volunteerism

2003: The *Boulder Daily Camera* selects her as a 2002 Pacesetter in the Quality of Life category for her long-term and far-reaching impact on volunteerism in her community.

Her Personal Life

Marlene was born in 1931 in Montana, where she spent many wonderful years in the small town of Nashua. She left in 1949 to go to Concordia College in Moorhead, Minnesota. There she met her future husband, Harvey. They were married in 1956 and lived in Pasadena and Costa Mesa, California. Their children, Richard and Lisa were born there. In 1968, they moved to Boulder, Colorado, to the same mountain home Marlene lives in today. Tragically, Harvey was killed in an accident in 1989 when he was just 58.

Her Volunteerism Philosophy

Marlene Wilson's basic philosophy about volunteerism is summed up in these few words (for which she was quoted by President George H. Bush during National Volunteer Week in 1991): "Caring must strengthen into commitment and commitment into action."

Introduction

from Marlene

Why am I publishing this book of some of my best speeches and workshops? I have at least three reasons. First, for years colleagues have been urging me to update and reissue my first book, *The Effective Management of Volunteer Programs.* Although much has changed since I wrote it in 1976, enough of the basic content remains relevant. But as I reviewed the many presentations I have made over the past 30 years, I realized that there was enough content here for a totally new book—and one that moves from a focus on "management" to a advocacy for *leadership*.

Second, as they just told you in the preceding Reflections essay, my two dear friends and colleagues, Jane Justis and Betty Stallings, have been urging me to do this for several years. They said, "We don't want to lose your stories, Marlene!" So, you'll find my anecdotes and parables liberally sprinkled throughout this book.

Finally, I've been thinking about some things I've read that spurred me on. Alex Haley, renowned author of the book, *Roots*, wrote about his trip to Africa to research his own family history. It was there he discovered the ancient custom of each tribal family having an oral historian called a *griot*. This person had memorized the family history and, on special family occasions, the historian would recite it. This role was passed on to a young person in each generation and that person became the living, talking history book for the family. Alex Haley said: "The experience brings the generations close, giving everyone a valuable sense of identity, interaction and belonging."

Max DePree, another author I like, also wrote about tribal storytelling in his book, *Leadership Is an Art:* "Every family, every college, every corporation, every institution needs tribal storytellers. The penalty for failing to listen is to lose one's history, one's historical context; one's binding values...people will begin to forget who they are."[1]

Harriet Naylor, considered by many to be the first to professionalize volunteer management through her advocacy on our behalf with the Federal government, was one who played the valuable role of griot for me when I first entered the field as a rookie in 1968. There have been many others as well and I'd like to play that role now, for those of you new to the field. I feel the time to do so is appropriate right now, as the profession of volunteer administration is struggling to re-define and rediscover itself. The impetus for this was the dissolution of our national professional association, the Association for Volunteer Administration (AVA) that went bankrupt in 2006. There are exciting efforts underway to establish a new and even better association and I'm sure this will happen in the next couple of years. It's vitally important that it does!

Since many of the keynote speeches I've included in this book were given at AVA national conferences over the past three decades, I hope this collection will help preserve some of the history of our profession and the field of volunteerism. Those were years of great challenge and change and we helped a baby profession grow and mature through it all.

I dedicate this book to all those colleagues who made it happen. It was a joy and privilege to work with such dedicated and loving people. I hope this book helps each reader develop "a deep appreciation for the past, an enriched sense of the present and a joyous anticipation of the future."[2]

---

[1] Max DePree, *Leadership Is an Art* (Dell, 1990), 81.

[2] Sara Ban Breathnach, *Simple Abundance* (Grand Central Publishing, 1995).

Section I:
Leadership — *Beyond* the How-tos
of Volunteer Management

When I first began training in the 1970s, everyone was starved for "how-to information." The majority of the workshops I conducted were about developing and maintaining a volunteer management system. My first book, *The Effective Management of Volunteer Programs* (1974), was completely devoted to that topic. During that same decade the University of Colorado Volunteer Management Certification Program was born. (The program was the fruit of collaboration between Dr. Ivan Scheier, Harriet Naylor and me. I served as the program director for 25 years and am proud of the many national experts that came to Boulder each summer to train volunteer management professionals.) When the program began, it focused on how to take solid business management principles and apply them to the field of volunteer administration.

In 1970, I read an essay by Robert Greenleaf entitled, "Servant as Leader." It was about choosing a leadership style that enabled people to be their best. I was immediately drawn to the concept because to me, this is the ideal for volunteer managers—to help people be and do their best. From that time forward, I spent a significant amount of time thinking, speaking and writing to volunteer program managers about leadership. I realized that people were becoming hungry for more information than just the "nuts and bolts" of running a volunteer program. Managers of volunteers wanted to learn about developing their leadership and creative problem-solving skills.

If you are reading this book and call yourself a director of volunteers, manager of volunteer resources, volunteer program manager, or whatever title you choose, you need to start thinking of yourself as a *leader*. And, if you want to be an effective leader, you must deliberately and conscientiously work at developing your skills.

So, I offer you Section I of this book, drawing from many of my favorite and most requested presentations and workshops. I start out with "Musings of a Chronologically Gifted Crone" written after my sabbatical year in 1994. These "musings" are what I discovered after seriously burning out. As all of you know, burnout is a significant problem in our field. "Musings" is a very personal work and I decided to start out with this as a gentle reminder to all of you wonderful, dedicated professionals to take care of yourself first!

"The Case for Effective Management of Volunteer Programs" is a mini-course on how to run a volunteer program. It's a classic mini-lesson on the nuts and bolts of volunteer administration.

Next is "It's All about Leadership: Enabling Volunteers and Staff to Be at their Best." Here you'll learn about basic leadership styles and more about Robert Greenleaf's "servant leader." I also share personal stories of the enabling leaders I've experienced in my life.

"Motivation: Placing Right People in Right Jobs" was my most popular workshop ever. I introduced this speech as a workshop at the CU Level One Volunteer Management Certificate Program in 1974. It immediately became a hit and I was asked to present this same workshop all over the country. "Motivation" is one of my all-time most requested workshops and I've updated it many times over the years. I still apply the lessons learned from this course in my everyday life.

"Influencing Outcomes You Care About" developed as I became skilled in creating and leading things (founding a volunteer center, writing books, creating a university-level volunteer training program, establishing a publishing business, making audio and video programs, advocating for national organizations). If you have a vision or dream about starting something new or want to advocate for a change to your program, read this. You'll learn about creative problem-solving skills (an important leadership skill) and—once you've looked creatively at your problems—how to go about negotiating to make them happen.

"Polishing the Potential of Volunteer Staff/Teams" deals with an issue that, sadly, was a problem when I began consulting in the 1970s and continues to plague programs today.

"Perk up Your Presentations" is a workshop I developed for AVA later in my career and shares my tips and strategies for giving speeches, workshops and trainings. It comes from my experience giving presentations and keynote speeches around the globe for almost 40 years.

Finally, "What Are You Marketing? VISION Is the Job of Leadership" and "Leading with Soul and Vision" speak about the essential job leaders have to always hold up vision for their programs and how to pass that vision and "fire in the belly" on to everyone in the program.

All of my workshops focus on getting people to think about *why* they are doing something a particular way. It is my firm belief that the best managers are successful because they have taken the time to understand the principles, or the *whys,* of what they are doing. *How* one goes about accomplishing a particular task can rapidly change with technology, but the reason *why* you are doing it remains the same.

Musings of a
Chronologically Gifted Crone

Points of Light Foundation
- National Community Service Conference
Kansas City, MO, June 1995

I got the inspiration for this title in one of those "middle of the night flashes." It sounds better than "ramblings of an old lady." I've discovered friends and colleagues are intrigued and amused by it and saying things like "I can't wait to see what you'll do with it!" Well, you need to know—coming up with the title was a whole lot easier than deciding what to do with it!

As a writer and trainer, I'm fascinated with words, so let's start there—with the words from my title.

Musings: Reflections, wonderings, internal conversations about life and "stuff," more questions than answers. Robert Keck observes in his book, *Sacred Eyes*, "There are no experts in loving, no scholars of living. No doctors of human emotions and no gurus of the soul." [1]

Chronologically gifted: When I was doing a conference in Florida for an agency serving seniors, a gentleman came up to me at break and told me how much he hated being referred to as a senior. I asked him what he wanted to be called and he proudly drew himself up and said, "chronologically gifted." That made wonderful sense to me and I've used the term ever since. Having had so many miles on the trail helps me feel gifted because I've had a full share of life's good and bad experiences. That gives one perspective.

Crone: Society's image of a crone tends to be a wizened, wrinkled old witch with a wart on her nose, but Marion Woodman defines a crone as

The "crone-in-training" delivering a speech.

...the truth teller at the crossroads — the wise woman who has gone through her many crossroads of life and has reached a place of conscious surrender where her ego demands are no longer relevant. She is not indifferent or withdrawn but totally present. She can be who she is and live her naked truth — to be a tuning fork to others.[2]

When I read that I became more than a little intimidated about the word crone being in my title—until I realized it's simply my goal and, if I live to be 150, I might attain it. In the meantime, I'd feel much better if you would all add a parenthesis after the word crone on the title page that reads "in training." The year of 1994 was a sabbatical year for me and I believe my sabbatical was an intentional commitment to begin my journey toward that goal.

The reason I even thought of doing a session like this is due to the many questions I kept getting both during and after my sabbatical:

- What is a sabbatical? Is it just another term for long vacation?
- What did you do on yours?
- Why did you take it instead of just retiring?
- What did you learn?
- Has it made a difference? If so, how?

People would add: We need more from you now than teaching volunteer management skills and how-tos. Share "life skills"—that's what we're hungry for. I did not want to tackle that assignment for it seemed both awesome and arrogant. But then came the title in the middle of the night and I was hooked. So here goes…

I find myself using images and metaphors more and more to illustrate concepts. In fact, one reason I went on sabbatical was my failure to see stories around me anymore. I was too busy and too stressed (40 cities in one year and the life of packing and unpacking, airplanes and hotels left little time or energy for that). Instead of defining a sabbatical, let me share a true story that serves as a fitting metaphor for mine.

In May, two dear friends and I went to Mexico for a week at a "fat farm," more glamorously known as a spa. (As you can see, my body got the message wrong and put fat **on** rather than took it off, but that's another story!)

On the very first day my friend, Arlene, and I decided we were going to take the meadow walk, described as a 2-mile intermediate trek. But, we didn't want to do it with the whole group as we are independent, loner types. The staff assured us the trail was well marked with signs and we'd have no trouble following it on our own.

Off we went expecting a pleasant, predictable and moderately taxing walk. What the staff failed to tell us was there were also big, white arrows painted on the ground going in the opposite direction for a 10K run later in the day. We followed the arrows instead of the signs and ended up doing a 10K up mountains, down valleys, six times across a mountain stream. All the time we expected the ranch to be right around the next bend. We had **no** idea where we were, but we were quite clear this was no two-mile meadow walk. Finally, we arrived at our destination, exhausted, but exhilarated. It had been a real challenge, and we loved it.

That experience sums up my sabbatical year. A tougher journey than I expected, full of surprises, ups and downs I'd never anticipated with health and family crises, valleys of despair, mountain top experiences, and crossing and re-crossing the same questions over and over and over.

And, one other and perhaps the most important part of the metaphor—when I had to cross that rushing mountain stream, balancing unsteadily on rocks to get across, it was Arlene's steadying and gentle hand offered to me that helped me make it. I hope that's what I can offer to you in this session: a gentle and reassuring hand of support as you cross your own streams.

One of the greatest benefits of taking time out is to reexamine, reflect on, and possibly reframe some of our basic paradigms of life. Paradigms are simply the lens we see things through; our belief systems that filter the information and data we choose to take in; the perceptual map we use to determine where we're going and how we'll get there.

Changing paradigms is a tougher job than I anticipated, because it goes to the core of who we are as opposed to what we do. To help me tackle this, I finally got serious about early morning quiet time and journaling. The pages of my journal became the place I engaged in serious dialog with myself, God, and others about my paradigms and questions.

I'd like to share a few of the paradigms that I have reaffirmed, shifted or am in the process of working on as they relate to:

- Our field of volunteer administration
- Work
- Health and wholeness
- Time and priorities
- Balance
- Quality of life

The Field of Volunteer Administration

The major question to deal with here is *why*? Why has this field evolved over the past three decades? For what unique purpose?

Since I have been an integral part of this evolution for 25 years (and busily churning out books, tapes and workshops to prove it), I was startled by how long it had been since I'd re-examined the critical *why* questions. To do so, I went back to a statement made 30 years ago in a speech given by one of the great wise women crones in my life, Harriet Naylor, a true pioneer in this field. She stated: "If doctors are concerned with health and lawyers with justice as their ideal; then I believe our profession is concerned with freedom of choice... I believe freedom is our responsibility."

As I pondered that, I realized with a start that much of the health care crisis is because doctors have shifted their focus away from health and onto illness. And, after watching even snatches of sensational trials (like the O.J. Simpson trial of 1994) one really has to question whether lawyers are still mainly concerned with justice, rather than theatrics. So, how about those of us in volunteer management? Are we still committed to freedom of choice? Do we still believe that freedom is our responsibility? Or is it all about products and power and numbers of slots and techniques and information?

We are no longer in the developmental stage of an emerging profession. So the question would seem to be: Can we move into the *influential* stage of a maturing profession and stay true to our ideal of freedom? This would seem to me to be an excellent goal for our profession, as well as for us as individuals.

In my opinion, this particular period in our nation's history is a challenging and often disturbing time for all of us who are in the human service professions. Programs we have initiated, nurtured and dedicated years to are being downsized or cut altogether. We have to make tough choices regarding how we respond. On our bad days, we find ourselves being mad as hell, scared to death, frustrated to tears, or totally resigned (and a job at Wal-Mart begins looking better and better).

Or, we can take a long hard look at the fact that in spite of all the funds, staff and volunteers we've thrown at community problems we haven't solved them. They've gotten worse. So do we fold up our tents and go to work at Wal-Mart? I don't think so. We learn to reframe and create new solutions.

So, what for us in volunteer administration? Our coming-of-age period has taught us much, both about what works and what does not when involving volunteers in meeting community problems. We are now entering a period pregnant with possibilities for our experience to make the difference between success and failure as more and more needs begin coming back to states and communities to solve.

What we know and do has never been more important to the survival of our democracy than at this very moment in history, for it will take the best and most creative thinking of staff, clients and volunteers to survive the coming years. Are we ready to re-commit to our unique paradigm of purpose? If so, roll up your sleeves and hang on for the roller coaster ride of your life as we help forge new coalitions of caring and replace turfdoms with teams.

Work

In one of the most thought-provoking books I've read lately, *The Heart Aroused*, David Whyte explores the vital task of recognizing that what is killing too many people at work is not so much the pace we go at but that we have removed the soul from our work. (He defines "soul" as "the indefinable essence of a person's spirit and being... It is not about functions, it is about beauty, form and memory.") He goes on to say: "While we think we are simply driving to work every morning to earn a living, the soul knows it's secretly engaged in a life-or-death struggle for its existence."[3]

Quite honestly, that was my most compelling reason for taking a sabbatical. I sensed I was in grave danger of the soul going out of my work. Did that mean it was simply time for me to quit (25 years is a long run on any stage) or should I retire and just enjoy myself (people told me I deserved to do that)? Was there another kind of work or career out there that could rekindle the "fire in the belly" excitement I'd had for this field for so long, or was it possible to somehow fan the embers and rekindle the flame for my work in this field?

I kept hoping and praying for the writing in the sky magic answer. I diligently read and wrote and pondered and probed, searching my psyche and my soul for the answer. And the most amazing thing finally happened...I quietly realized that I knew the answer. And it seemed quite unspectacular (no firecrackers, sky writing, symphonies or anything).

The experience and my answer can best be described by sharing a similar quest of a woman described in the book *Sacred Eyes* by Robert Keck. It's a true story of his wife, Diana, (a teacher, psychotherapist and business woman who had reached the same crossroads of purpose as I did). Her answer came in a powerful dream, she writes:

> *I was with a woman who appeared to be my teacher. I listened carefully as she explained the value of releasing old energy patterns. She said there was really nothing wrong with the energy I was carrying around except for the fact that it was old, stale and flat. The energy flowing through my activity had lost its sparkle and the vitality it once had.*
>
> *In a ritualistic manner, my teacher began to remove old patterns from my life: the old images, the old objects, and the old feelings, while simultaneously replacing them with exact but renewed replicas. I did not look any different and externally my life did not appear changed. But at the energetic level everything was transformed. The changes were subtle but I began to experience a deeper and clearer connection to all that surrounded me. Despair was replaced with hope, and depression was replaced with a vibrant and hopeful faith in a renewed future.[4]*

Since many of you have told me that you, too, are feeling burned out and uncertain about your work and future (in volunteer administration, or any other career) let's take a few moments for you to explore two questions:

1. Why did I enter this profession in the first place?
2. Why have I stayed?

The answers to these two questions may lead you to the third and most critical question:

3. Do I still want to be in it?

What helped me to finally realize that I truly did want to fan the embers, blow on the coals and stay in this field is when I realized I am still totally committed to what I believe this work is all about and why I've loved it for so many years.

What do I believe our field has to give to others that is ours uniquely? To give hope! These are angry, confusing, violent times of change and transition. People feel overwhelmed and lost. Too many feel they have no control over their lives and no impact on others.

Volunteering, when it's done well, can be an antidote to people's feelings of alienation and hopelessness. When people volunteer, they experience firsthand that they can make a difference in other people's lives and especially when they join with others taking back responsibility and control of their own communities and neighborhoods. They begin to see and experience the good in themselves and others. This is democracy at its best!

A late dear friend and colleague of many of us in this field, Mary Wiser, sent this wonderful piece to me and I'd like to share it.

A Sufi Teaching Story

Past the seeker as he prayed came the crippled and the beggar and the beaten.

Seeing them, the holy one went down into deep prayer and cried. "Great God, how is it that a loving creator can see such things and yet do nothing about them?"

And, out of the long silence the voice of God gently and challengingly spoke. "I did do something. I made you!"

As Whyte says in *The Heart Aroused*, "knowing why we build and when to build and if to build then has a bedrock importance for us. Our lives depend on it...The marvelous peculiarity about admitting to being lost is that we come to our senses. We wake up. We look around with a keenness we didn't have before."[5]

Health/Wholeness

For years I fell into the common American trap of thinking of health as simply the absence of illness and I considered myself a healthy person and was thankful for that. A once-a-year check up and some sinus medication was the extent of my medical costs. Friends and family often said "you never get sick!" and my answer was "I don't have time!" I am slowly realizing health is really about wholeness and includes our physical, mental, emotional, spiritual and relational condition. Let's look at each for a moment:

Physical:

Let me use another metaphor from nature to illustrate my biggest "a-ha" about this vital aspect of health.

I live in the mountains outside of Boulder and one night I was awakened by a strange crashing sound in my living room. My bedroom is on the floor above it and when I turned on the light and looked over the balcony railing there was a huge raccoon in the middle of my living room. He had fallen down the chimney into my fireplace. He scrambled out and was looking for an escape route. I ran down the stairs, grabbed a broom and chased him from room to room for several minutes. Finally I realized all my doors were closed so on my next sprint around the house I opened every door and shortly he dashed out to freedom. I honestly don't know which of us was more surprised or scared by the whole incident.

It occurred to me that health problems are often like raccoons invading our living rooms—they get our full attention and drain our energy until we deal with them. Oddly enough, I spent more on health-related issues during my one-year sabbatical than during the previous ten years put together. My body needed to get my attention—and it did!

Raccoon #1:

It started almost as soon as my sabbatical began with a "mock heart attack" that resulted in an ambulance ride down from my condo in the mountains to the ICU unit for two days. The doctor finally decided it had been a spasm of my esophagus. My son, Rich, with his wonderfully wry humor said, "You mean all that was because you had gas?"

Raccoon #2:

Then came what appeared to be a severe asthma attack (checked out negative) but I still had trouble breathing.

Granddaddy raccoon #3:

Then the really big raccoon landing in my living room when I discovered there was a fatal gene running around my family tree for Huntington's Disease. After making the painful decision to have the test to learn if I had it or not, it took five months to wait for the results. Fortunately, I don't have the gene, so my kids can't get it either, but during this process I learned much about never again taking health or life for granted. Living each day to the fullest and being very clear about priorities.

Raccoon #4:

This fellow literally landed on my head. I took a freak fall and nearly scalped myself. (This happened only a week after getting the good news about Huntingdon's Disease.) I ended up with 36 stitches sewing "my lid" back on and a clear reminder that not only illness, but also accidents can be a wake-up call.

You can begin to see why answering people's question, "What did you do on your sabbatical?" has been hard to do. The easy part is to tell about my cruise to Alaska, my walking tour of Vermont in the fall, seeing six New

York plays, my family trip to Lake Tahoe, and my writing retreat to Cape Cod. Those were all wonderful and the needed fun part of my journey...but they're not the whole story, as you can see.

Mental Renewal

This came easier for me as I'm a reader by nature and a learner by design. I read 25-30 nonfiction books plus over 50 novels for fun and relaxation. What a treat! And, I attended (as a participant, not presenter) several conferences, just for me! Max DePree, Stephen Covey, Ken Blanchard, Maya Angelo, Ram Dass and M. Scott Peck to name a few. These reinforced many beliefs I've held for a long time regarding leadership, empowerment, team building and management and triggered new ideas and approaches. They helped replenish my mental and intellectual storehouse which I knew had run pretty dry the past few years.

Emotional/Spiritual

Here's where the hardest work was needed: I'd shut down feelings to survive over the past few years. It was about loss and grief, the deaths of my husband, mother, sister, favorite aunt, cousin, and a good friend.

I used journaling to re-connect with the feeling part of me and it was painful, but very healing. Two wonderful books guided me: *The Artist's Way* by Julia Cameron and *Life's Companion* by Christina Baldwin.

It occurred to me after a vivid dream, what the first two raccoon (health) episodes were all about. The dream was that I woke up from a sound sleep and found I couldn't move because there was a giant rock sitting on my chest. I could hardly breathe. A-ha! Heart/asthma/breathing. Could they be related to the emotional rock I'd fashioned to protect myself that was keeping me from moving on—to get beyond surviving to thriving? It sounded very plausible but, how to get rid of the rock?

I started by intentionally being aware of every time I wrote the phrase "I think" in my journal. I would cross it out and write "I feel" and name how I felt. It may sound like kindergarten steps but it worked for me. Also, every time I wrote "I ought" or "I should," I crossed it out and wrote "I want." I recommend this to all you rescuers of the world out there...it was quite amazing how hard that was and how helpful.

Then came a profound insight from Christina Baldwin, my teacher at the writing retreat. I told her in a private session about my rock dream and said, "It's sitting right on my heart and keeps me from getting deeper, to the soul in my work. How do I chip away at this rock? Do I have to peel it off one layer at a time by revisiting all the grief and dealing with it?" I felt that would be like scraping away with a teaspoon and I was overwhelmed at the prospect.

Christina is a very eclectic, new age spiritual person and she smiled and said "I think there's a story somewhere about a rock being rolled away." And here I was, a Christian all my life and I'd forgotten it! That's what happened, the rock rolled away and I can breathe again! I can feel again, too.

U.S. author, editor, and radio host Clifton Fadiman, in commenting about one of our society's most prevalent feelings, boredom, describes it this way: "not unhappiness, not fatigue…but that odd modern stunned look that comes from a surplus of toys and a deficiency of thoughts." He goes on to suggest that to be a whole person, two things are essential:

- A faith to live by
- A cause to live for

I wrote in my journal at one point:

I must remember my center is my spiritual life. My faith in a God who loves me (and the world) is what anchors me in times of uncertainty and chaos and is my touchstone in times of decision and change. My challenge is to keep experiencing this God as mystery and never try to shrink Him to fit into my own limitations of understanding but to keep exploring and questioning for as long as I live.

Relational

If I had been addressing these elements of wholeness in order of priority, I would have put this one first without a doubt for, in sorting out the important from the urgent when determining life priorities, what could possibly be more important than family and friends?

What I learned in my months off was how easy it is to take relationships for granted and how important it is to nurture them with attention and intentional quality time. We put them at the top of the "to-do" list as wants (and not as "oughts" and "shoulds" or "when I find a moment"). It's about having a personal support system. I've come to realize over the years that there are several different kinds of relationships within the general category of friendships:

Acquaintances:

These are casual relationships. Surface conversation usually centers on activities and facts instead of feelings (i.e., "what are you doing now?"). Since we're all in the people business we have dozens of acquaintances.

Friends:

These are people who really want to know "how are you?" and with whom you share core feelings and mutual interests and activities. You enjoy being together.

Intimates:

Those precious few who really want to know what is in your heart and soul, what are the questions you're grappling with and the joys you're discovering. They love and support you, no matter what! They accept you, warts and all. You don't have to fit any role for them, just be who you really are. I've been privileged to have a few of these precious relationships over the years and value them enormously. In fact, I cannot even imagine how I could have survived the past few years without them.

I feel especially blessed because my two adult children, Rich and Lisa, are also intimate friends to me. During my sabbatical, they were among those who offered gentle steadying hands to help me across the white water. They had both taken a sabbatical and knew about the currents, eddies and black holes along the way. They were valued guides and teachers.

Support groups:

Besides the important self-help groups that so many people have found invaluable in dealing with particular problems or issues there is another kind of group I'd like to mention. That is where a small group of people (usually six or less) come together to form a mutual support group. It has the same level of sharing as intimate friends and provides a sort of synergistic sharing of hopes, dreams, disappointments, successes, fears and fun—but mostly just the joy of being together. These have been among life's greatest gifts to me.

But strangely enough I realized I did not have such a support group in my own home town though I'd lived there almost 30 years. I was gone as much as I was there. So that was another intentional goal of my sabbatical and I didn't have a clue how to start. Then a dear friend in Boulder brought together a group of six women whom she knew (but we didn't know each other). It was an uncommon group on the surface: a CPA, a national hospice counselor/ trainer, a dream group leader, a massage therapist, a house cleaner (who was an ex-nun and nurse) and me. Our common denominator was we were all on a spiritual quest of some kind and we all were friends of Barbara.

We've met bi-weekly now for over a year and have become bonded in an unbelievable closeness. To illustrate how strange and mysterious are the ways of life, one-and-a-half months ago Barbara was diagnosed with terminal brain cancer. Our group has become her primary care givers (as she has no local family). Does it strike you as awesome that all the skills needed are right there—financial, nursing, counseling, spiritual advisor and volunteer coordinator? It's been one of the most potent reminders I've ever had about priorities and friends and what life's really all about. If there's only one thing you carry away from this session, I hope it will be the importance of creating and nurturing a personal support system. Move it to the top of your priority list—for your sake!

A great example of how support groups can provide both fun and profit is the Beardstown Ladies Investment Group. Fifteen women from a small Iowa town, ages 40s - 80s, came together in 1982 to educate themselves about stocks and investments. But what they found along the way was the enjoyment and enrichment of being together. They adopted the slogan "use it or lose it!" Financially their stock portfolio has earned an average annual return of 23%

over the past decade. They have wowed Wall Street, produced best-selling books and videos, been on most of the national talk shows and are having the time of their lives.

Quality of Life

Paying Attention

Living life to the fullest is, first of all, about paying attention! Do any of you fall into the trap I so often do when I'm running at full steam?

- I look but don't really see.
- I listen but don't recall what I hear.
- I taste but don't really savor.
- I experience but don't really feel.
- I read but don't really learn.
- I smile but don't really laugh.
- I pray but don't really trust.

It occurred to me that's not being in the fast lane of life, it's being on the shoulder. And as we all know, driving on the shoulder can be very dangerous indeed.

I was struck at how many of the authors I read stressed the vital importance of paying attention to the moment, living fully in the present (versus fretting about the past or anticipating the future). What we have is now and the question is: What is the best use of my energy and time right now?

Balance

Remember how we used to teeter-totter as kids? The trick was learning to shift our weight and positions so we could balance just above the ground. For helping professionals like us, I think every day becomes a balancing act between:

Self . . . . Others
Being. . . . . Doing
Feeling . . . . Thinking
Work . . . . Play
Being with others . . . Solitude
My wants . . . . Oughts / Shoulds
Laughter. . . . . Tears

It takes skill and attention to keep our teeter-totters balanced, at least part of the time. It's a worthy goal for all of us who are truly committed to wholeness and health.

Replenishing

One of the most meaningful experiences I had at the "fat farm" was a lesson in replenishing. The ranch grows all its own food and does so organically. One of our hikes was to the garden to see how they do it. The gardener explained to us the importance of crop rotation, knowing what each type of plant took from and returned to the soil based on the nature of that plant. They move the beds around so the soil is never depleted. There were five different compost beds which they selectively used to return what was needed to any bed (acid, nitrogen, fertilizer) before they replanted anything.

What a great analogy for our renewal. Where are you feeling depleted and burned out and what would replenish and nourish that in you? Is rotation in order?

Attitude

I have come to suspect that a sabbatical is probably more about intention and attitude then it is about a certain period of time. At least that feels true for me. Maybe I could define what I mean by this by sharing one last dream with you.

I don't know how many of you are familiar with Jung's notion that each person consists of a variety of internal persons (our many selves). I finally tried to identify and name some of mine and one of my dominate characters is "the general." I envision him in full uniform full of ribbons and always issuing me orders. He's no doubt why I've been able to juggle my complex schedule the past few years. I knew I'd have to tame my general if I was going to be able to slow down my pace.

My first dream about the general was part way into my sabbatical. I saw him at the end of a large auditorium seated at what looked like a huge computer. But as I got close, I saw that although he was still in uniform his tie was off, his shirt collar open and I was amazed that it wasn't a computer he was sitting at, rather he was playing magnificent music on a pipe organ.

He appeared in one more dream just before my sabbatical ended. A friend and I were at a summer camp and had gone off on an adventure and arrived back at the camp hours late. Waiting at the gate was my general only he was in khaki shorts and a t-shirt and when I apologized for being late he smiled and said "Oh, that's quite all right as long as you enjoyed yourself." Then he bent down and hugged me. If that wasn't a message from me to myself, I don't know what is! Now my challenge is to keep my new general in shorts and t-shirt even though I'm back in the midst of it all.

Summary

I'd like to return, in closing, to the crone. David Whyte said this about the crone:

She is the older woman who has given over priorities of pleasing husband and family in order to pass on a tested and tightly knit feminine wisdom to the world...She is the part of us that limps across the chasm when we cannot leap across.[6]

I love the image of limping because, as a crone-in-training, the only work I can truly be responsible for is the work on me. My internal work to determine who I am as a person, what I stand for and believe in and what I intend to do about that personally and professionally. That will always be "work in progress."

---

[1] L. Robert Keck, *Sacred Eyes* (Knowledge Systems, 1992).
[2] Marion Woodman, *Sitting by the Well* (Sounds True, 1991).
[3] David Whyte, *The Heart Aroused* (Doubleday, 1994), 13.
[4] Keck, op. cit., 216-217.
[5] Whyte, op. cit., 25.
[6] Ibid., 54.

The Case for Effective Management of Volunteer Programs

National Center for Voluntary Action (NCVA)
National Conference
Yale University, June 1982

I received a phone call the other day from an Associated Press reporter doing both an article and a book on "the changing world of volunteerism." He'd read my book, *The Effective Management of Volunteer Programs* and asked me if I felt the field had passed through the phase of management and was moving on to (or back to) "altruism and duty and all that good stuff." It was as though we'd gone through a catchy fad of some kind over the past ten years.

Just a couple of weeks before this incident I was confronted by a distraught volunteer director at a meeting. She'd been to a conference recently on volunteerism and the theme seemed to her to be that management is passé in the "new world of volunteerism." She was upset because she said she'd just spent the last two years developing better management skills and now "they" seemed to be saying that was out. (And, what really upset her was that she was personally discovering that her new-found management skills really worked!) She was confused.

I suspect that we are experiencing a new form of semantic game playing. Programs and organizations do not have the option of being managed or not managed. The opposite of effective management is *mis*management, not no management.

Here's the definition of management: *Working with and through others to accomplish goals.*

To have a program, project or organization, someone has to have a reason for bringing it into being (goal); call others together who also want that particular thing to happen (leaders); divide up the work to be done (organize, job descriptions); find people to help (staff, recruit). The only difference is some programs and organizations are much more effective at it than others. You cannot non-manage, you can only decide on different goals, styles and outcomes of how you do it.

So, when you hear that the newer forms of volunteerism (self-help and "neighborhood" groups are current buzz words) don't need management-centered "organized programs," don't believe it.

By the way, the opposite of organized is disorganized or unorganized. Have you ever tried to be involved in any group that fits that description?

Another myth is that our economy and shrinking resources are making managers of volunteers a luxury. They are being cut from budgets, as are state offices of volunteerism, and others. Tell me, those of you who have managed homes, is your job of home management easier or tougher in times of tight personal budgets versus times of plenty? When do you have to use your best skills to make things work? How do you make house payments, get the car fixed, go to dentist appointments, plan menus, and buy clothes for school?

How people can say we need less skill at management in these times of tight budgets and diminishing staff boggles my mind. It is totally illogical and dangerous. People today are struggling personally with their own tight budgets and busy schedules.

Mismanagement and disorganization are luxuries our volunteer and human service programs can ill afford. If we waste people's time we will lose their commitment and their involvement. People find time to volunteer today to make a difference and it is the job of each of us to get our acts together to make that possible. We are responsible for the world's most precious resource—people power.

So, you might say I'm a human environmentalist or a human resource conservationist, and I hope you are, too.

I suggest that the options we have in dealing with the ever changing world of today's manager can be likened to the options I have seen people choose in dealing with the waves of the ocean.

There are victims. Those who walk out into the waves; get knocked down; turn around and walk back into the waves; get knocked down; and on and on. They never seem to learn from their experiences and they don't seem to have much fun either.

There are floaters. They decide being knocked down by the waves doesn't make much sense so they get an inflatable air mattress which supports them above the waves. The turmoil of the waves goes on around them but they float on unconcerned. The only problem is they never go very far.

There are snorkelers. They become curious about what is going on beneath the waves. They rent snorkeling equipment and get totally absorbed in looking at the coral, rocks and fish. They become detached observers.

There are the surfers. These are the venturesome souls who have been victims, floaters or snorkelers at some point. But then they became convinced that there was more to dealing with the ocean than first meets the eye. They take surfing lessons from someone who knows how. They are not afraid of risks. They go out further into the ocean each time and they are also apt to fall off their boards, but they keep getting back on. The skill the successful surfer eventually learns is to discern which waves to let go by and which waves will take them all the way into shore, exactly where they want to go.

Organizations today need a great many more surfers. My hope is that I may help each of you become one.

Marlene presenting the functions of the volunteer manager in the early '80s.

The Volunteer Management System

As we begin to discuss the system, I have a startling observation to share with you. It may be controversial but I have given it a great deal of thought. My personal conviction is this: What we need to do to manage a successful volunteer program is exactly the same today as it was 25 years ago. I am speaking of the functions that we must carry out. I told you it was a shocker!

In this instamatic, turbulent, throw-away world how could anything stay the same over that period of time?

Let me add this crucial addendum: *How* we carry out these functions has changed dramatically to respond to the changing world in which we live and work. There are changes in the makeup of the volunteer work force, technology, downsizing and always new and different needs. The late columnist Sydney Harris once said, "We Americans are funny about change…we both love it and hate it. What we'd really like is for things to stay the same and get better." My friends, I think that's exactly what we are able to do if we hold fast to the essential framework of what we do but become flexible, creative and responsive to our changing world in how we get our work done.

Figure 1 shows the functions of the volunteer manager. It is important, in my opinion, that volunteer managers must see that each of these functions are done and done well. Delegation and staff training are necessary if this is to happen. It is also important to do them in order. There is an elegant and logical flow to the progression. It works, as it has for the past three decades.

Figure 1: Functions of a Manager

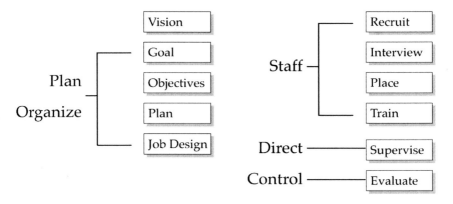

A common mistake is to start with recruitment, something new volunteer managers are often pressured to do. It's like trying to dance before the music begins. You will usually end up out of step. The key to sound management is matching the right people to the right jobs. To do that we must:

- Know why we need volunteers in the first place (planning).
- Know what skills, time and abilities we need (job descriptions).
- Know the interests, availability and skills of the volunteers (interviewing).

The *Hows* of Planning and Evaluation

Let's examine the Siamese twins of management, planning and evaluation, because they are often neglected. Planning is deciding in advance what to do, how to do it, when to do it and who is to do it. Planning bridges the gap from where we are to where we want to go. Evaluation is deciding if where we have gone is in fact where we intended to go.

Let me share a true story. Years ago, I worked in a mental hospital where a patient spent many busy days knitting a dress. The problem was that although she knew how to knit, she had no plan or pattern for a dress. So day after day she knit, always expecting it to come out looking like the dress she envisioned. In reality, it was just a very long scarf, getting longer and longer by the day. She refused advice or help, stating adamantly that she knew what she was doing and didn't need any busybodies telling her how to do what she had done for years. It was not until she decided to try on her dress that she realized it had not turned out as she expected. And, the biggest tragedy was that she could not understand why it didn't turn out.

Have you ever seen organizations knit "non-programs" and not know it? It's sad, but avoidable with careful planning and evaluation.

To be honest most of us think we are better at planning than we really are. The humorous columnist Erma Bombeck has four questions to check out personal planning abilities:

1. *Can you put your hands on the Christmas cards you bought at half price last January?*
2. *Do you use candles at your house for romantic atmosphere or simply because you forgot to pay the light bill last month?*
3. *Do you usually get all of the items on your daily to-do list accomplished or do you spend most of your time walking around asking what day it is?*
4. *When you go grocery shopping do you have time to put the groceries into the cupboard or do you eat directly from the car?*

Let's go through the planning process, step-by-step.

Step 1: Vision

Where are you going? What is the preferred future for your volunteer program? Where do you want to be 5-10 years from now?

Step 2: Mission/Purpose

What business are you in? What problems are you trying to solve? Why do you exist as an organization or program? You must begin with the mission of your organization and if you aren't clear about what that is, be sure you get it in writing as soon as possible.

Here's an example:

The Problem: More and more women and children are being forced into homelessness in this community every year.

A Sample Mission Statement: The mission of the XYZ Agency is to alleviate the problems of homelessness for women and children in this city.

Next you need to define the mission of your volunteer program in terms of how it helps your organization achieve its mission. This is extremely important if you want to establish credibility with your administration and staff. Extend and enrich the work of paid staff in service of your client.

Sample Volunteer Program Mission Statement: The mission of the XYZ volunteer program is to mobilize the extensive resources of this community to assist this agency in meeting the needs of homeless women and children.

Step 3: Objectives/Goals

What does the volunteer program intend to do about your mission this year? What are your 5-6 major priorities? State these in measurable, achievable terms and be sure they're compatible with the mission of the organization and your program.

Goals for XYZ Agency Volunteer Program

1. Develop a volunteer recruitment task force by September 1 of this year to recruit:
   - Fifty volunteers from churches and service clubs by year-end to help staff our two shelters during evening hours.
   - Ten to fifteen high school and college students to begin a tutoring program for children in our shelters by next November 1.
   - Twenty-five short-term volunteers to help build three Habitat for Humanity homes between July and October of next year.
   - Six to eight corporate and community leaders by year-end to serve on a task force with our staff to explore establishing a job training and placement service for our clients.
   - Two advocacy volunteers by September 1 to research legislation regarding low-income housing issues to help staff prepare for budget hearings.

2. Design and implement a staff training program regarding their roles and responsibilities when using volunteers.

3. Evaluate and re-design our volunteer training program by next March.

Tip: You must acknowledge the wide variety of skills your volunteers are providing to your program. This helps to change your staff's perception about the value and scope of your program.

Step 4: Action Plans

Action plans deal with these questions:

- Who will be responsible for each objective?
- How will they accomplish it?
- When is it due and what is the necessary time line to ensure completion?
- What costs will be entailed? To whom will you delegate?

Here is an example of an action plan:

Objective: Form a volunteer recruitment task force.
Goal: Recruit 10-15 student volunteer tutors.
Paid Staff: Director of Volunteers
Responsibilities: Recruit a volunteer to head up the task force and delegate responsibilities to the task force.

Volunteer Director ➝ Volunteer Director and Joe Rush

WHO	HOW	WHEN	COST
Volunteer Head of Task Force Joe Rush: Retired School Teacher	Contact education depart- Explore possibility of students receiving credit for tutoring	By 9/15/xx	Books and school supplies
	Talk to high school principals for referrals. Recruit 1 high school and 1 college student as recruiters (for more tutors)	By 9/30/xx	
	Make presentations in appropriate classes	Sept. and October	Transportation Meals for tutors

Step 5: Job Design

Job design is about determining all the work that needs to be done and dividing it into "doable" pieces of work. You are defining *what* not *how*. *Figure 2* shows a sample job description form.

Figure 2: Sample Job Description Forms

Most Responsible Volunteer Position

Title: Volunteer Recruitment Task Force Leader (or Chairman)

Responsible to: Director of Volunteers

Area of Responsibility: To be responsible for the recruitment of volunteers for this agency. This includes the organization of other volunteers to assist in this outreach effort as needed; the design of recruitment materials; and the implementation of recruitment objectives, as defined together with the Director of Volunteers and approved by the Advisory Committee.

Length of Commitment: One (1) year.

Qualifications: Organizational skills, knowledge of public relations and ability to work well with staff and other volunteers. Knowledge of community is helpful.

Comments: This position carries a good deal of responsibility and thus it is recommended that it be your only (or at least, major) volunteer commitment for this year.

————————————Less Responsible Volunteer Position————————————

Title: Speaker's Bureau Volunteer

Responsible to: Volunteer Recruitment Task Force Leader

Definition of Duties: Give presentations and/or speeches on behalf of this agency for the purpose of recruiting more volunteers and encouraging community support of our organization and its goals. Speeches to be given at service clubs, churches and other interested groups as assigned by Recruitment Task Force Leader.

Time Required: 2-4 hours per month. Generally audiences would meet over lunch or dinner hours, but not always.

Qualifications: Public speaking; ability to operate visual aid equipment helpful. Commitment to agency's goals and objectives and a belief in the value of volunteers. Enthusiasm a must!

Training Provided: Orientation sessions will be arranged with staff and volunteers to thoroughly acquaint volunteer with this agency, the volunteer program and the needs of both.

————————————Least Responsible Volunteer Position————————————

Title: Telephone Aide

Responsible to: Volunteer Recruitment Task Force Leader and Secretary

Definition of Duties: Telephone prospective volunteers from lists obtained at speeches and presentations to set up interviews with the staff. Phoning should be done from the Office of Volunteers.

Time Required: 2 hours a week. Monday morning preferred.

Qualifications: Pleasant phone personality and ability to work congenially with staff and volunteers.

Comments: This volunteer must have transportation available, as our agency is not accessible by public transportation.

When you create volunteer job positions think in terms of these three levels of jobs:

- Most responsible
- Less responsible
- Least responsible

You do this because your volunteers bring different skills and talents to your organization and also have varying limits to the amount of time they can devote to the job.

Step 6: Recruitment

We now know more about who is out there and what's going on in their lives. Now let's get practical about how you can recruit the new volunteers for your program.

Redefine Recruitment

Instead of "oughts" and "shoulds" and "your turn" and arm twisting, how about thinking of recruitment as marketing? When you think of recruitment in this way new behaviors and creative ideas start to flow and make recruitment fun!

Also, I like to think of recruitment as "an invitation" to come and talk about our organization's needs and opportunities and the recruitee's dreams, gifts and vision.

Here are some images that come to my mind when thinking of recruitment in this way:

- Personal—not "addressed to occupant."
- Something is happening—not "sorry, I can't get anyone to come."
- RSVP—we both decide.

Compare this to images of the "old" approach:

- "You're the last on my list and we're desperate."
- White lies: "There's really nothing to it, it will hardly take any time."
- Guilt.

There is one catch to using this approach. If you believe in recruitment as "an invitation to come and talk," then someone in your organization must always be ready and trained to talk to volunteers when they initiate contact.

Think marketing

You are marketing your cause (your mission) when you recruit. Always remember *your mission is your strongest recruitment tool*. Be sure you know what yours is and make it motivating!

Choose your recruiters (marketers) carefully. They should have these characteristics:

- Believe in and are excited about your cause.
- Have personal experience with your organization either as staff, volunteers or clients.
- Are not burned out.
- Can speak the language and have credibility with the group they're trying to reach.

Target your market

Understand whom you're trying to reach and their blocks to saying "yes." Blocks may include timing, babysitting, transportation, etc. Think of creative ways to remove these blocks and you'll get more "yes" replies.

Your recruitment plan

Recruitment should be year-round and varied. Try to avoid one-shot recruitment done at the last minute. Here are four questions to ask yourself when creating a recruitment plan:

- Whom are you trying to recruit?
- Where will you find them?
- How can you communicate with them?
- What will you say and how will you say it?

Step 7: Interviewing

First a definition: I think of interviewing as "inner viewing"—a conversation with a purpose, more than a friendly chat. It can be fun when done properly because it gives you the opportunity to get to know a person as a person, a rare thing in our society. Good interviewing requires a mixture of acquired skills and using your intuition.

These are some common types of interviews:

- **Screening:** This happens in the volunteer office. Is the volunteer really interested in helping our particular cause?
- **Placement:** After screening, the program director interviews the volunteer to determine the best placement. Here you are looking for clues to the volunteer's style and values and determining where he or she will best fit into your organization.

In my opinion, interviewing skills are some of the most important skills any leader will ever develop. Why?

- They help you choose right people for right jobs.
- Volunteers don't need or deserve failure—they deserve success.
- Our clients/members must be protected. Screening and interviewing are the first line of defense in risk management.

- There is no better public relations tool than a satisfied volunteer. Conversely, a dissatisfied volunteer can be a public relations nightmare.
- The morale of other volunteers and paid staff is at stake.

There are four critical components to an interview:

1. The climate you set.
2. The questions you ask and how you ask them.
3. How you listen.
4. How you follow up.

Here are some sample questions **about skills/interests/gifts** to have in your repertoire:

- What skills do you wish you could learn?
- What interesting things have you done in the past either as a volunteer or paid staff?
- What have you done that's given you the greatest satisfaction?
- What do you feel you're good at? Might be good at? Not good at?
- Have you tried anything new lately? How did it go?

Here are some questions about involvement:

- How do you feel about your current level of involvement?
- Would you prefer more, less or different kinds of involvement?
- *If an active volunteer:* What do you like/dislike about what you're doing right now? Is it worth the effort?
- *If an inactive volunteer:* What would have to change in your life for you to become active again?

Here are some other interviewing tips:

- If the volunteer is limited by age or health ask questions like: "What comes easily to you?"
- If the potential volunteer seems defensive, emphasize the past; it's safer.
- If the potential volunteer is uncommunicative, try a different angle.
- To draw out teens, ask them about school, after-school activities and past experiences.

Step 8: Training

Training involves equipping people to succeed in the things they've said "yes" to. The extent of training needed and how to best deliver it depends on the past experience of the volunteer and the job to be done.

Step 9: Supervision

Your leadership style determines how you do this and how others feel about working with you. I like this quote from an unknown source:

As leaders we need to be more like gardeners than manufacturers. We need to grow instead of make people. When you want tomatoes, you plant tomato seeds, carefully choose the right soil and place and then take care of them. We don't make tomatoes, we allow them to grow.

Part of good supervision is **recognition**. How do we let volunteers know that we noticed and cared about what they've done?

Step 10: Evaluation

In evaluation, we determine our "well dones" and our "opportunities to improve." For example, did we achieve all of our objectives for the year? Were we on time and within budget? If not, why not? How did volunteers, staff and clients feel about our program? (You will need to do interviews and surveys to determine this.) How do we feed this information into our next planning process?

When you are planning, evaluating or re-evaluating keep these essential points in mind:

- It is vitally important to plan *with* not *for* people. Pin this up on your wall if you have to. People become committed to plans they help make.
- Keep planning as simple and concise as possible.
- Continually delineate between the important and the urgent. Setting priorities when writing your objectives helps you concentrate your resources on the vital few outcomes that will have the most impact on your volunteer program. Otherwise you end up doing a little bit of everything but doing nothing well.
- Have patience and persistence. A fully operational, effective volunteer system takes 3-5 years to develop. Keep honing, creating and perfecting as you go.
- Be sure evaluations are fed back into your next planning cycle:
   o Know what went well and keep doing it.
   o Know what did not go well and determine why, then change it or drop it.
   o Determine what was needed that you did not accomplish and add to the next set of priorities.

Retention

Finally, I'd like to talk about retention. Retention is important to all volunteer organizations. In my years directing a volunteer program I developed these eight keys to strengthening volunteer retention:

1. Clear expectations
2. Meaningful work
3. Adequate training, supervision and staff support
4. Opportunities for growth and change
5. Meaningful recognition
6. Understanding current profile of volunteers
7. Receptive climate
8. Compatible organizational culture

So, that's my mini effective management of volunteers workshop. Elizabeth O'Conner is a favorite author of mine. In her book, *Search for Silence,* she states the magnitude of our mission so well: "To be in earnest about a vision is to think about strategy—how to take what is out in the distance and bring it into the here and now where it can be perceived by ordinary sight."[1]

I believe the time for well-managed volunteer programs has come and my fervent prayer is that our volunteer programs will leap, not limp into the years ahead.

---

[1] Elizabeth O'Connor, *Search for Silence* (Word Books, 1974), 106.

It's All About Leadership: Enabling Volunteers and Staff to Be at Their Best

Two Speeches Combined
Association for Volunteer Administration Annual Conferences
Seattle, WA, 1985 and Kansas City, MO, 1990

The art of leadership is liberating people to do what is required of them in the most effective and humane way possible…it begins with a belief in the potential of people. Participative management without a belief in that potential and without conviction about the gifts people bring to organizations is a contradiction in terms.

—Max DePree, *Leadership Is an Art*

When you find yourself in a leadership position, you have many important decisions you need to make. The most important one is what kind of leadership style you choose to practice. Your leadership style will dramatically affect all who work with and for you.

Here are the typical leadership styles:

The Boss: The boss makes all significant decisions. He decides and tells everyone what to do. It's a traditional leadership style that is becoming less and less effective in today's society.

The Expert: The expert leader acts as if she "knows all significant things." People look to her as the know-it-all and she doesn't let on that she doesn't know it all.

The Doer: The doer leader "does all the significant things." Doers don't delegate, they do it all themselves. Doer leaders don't let anyone under them grow or develop.

The Hero/Martyr: Hero/martyr leaders like to tell everyone how awful everything is, like the expression: "It feels so good to feel so bad." They are miserable to work with because they are very verbal with their problems.

The Abdicrat: The abdicrat leaders retire without leaving. They hold onto their position but don't do anything with it.

The Enabler/Servant Leader: The servant-leader style is committed to enabling other people.

I was struck by the servant-leader style when I first read Robert Greenleaf's 1970 essay, "Servant as Leader."[1] It fit in with my philosophy about volunteer management and particularly my concern, which has been growing since the mid-1970s, that volunteer managers needed to realize their roles as leaders and think about their own leadership styles. Key features of this style include:

- Gets program goals met with and through other people. The servant leader is a "people grower."
- Enables other people to succeed.
- Sees jobs in do-able parts, finds the right people to do the parts and then provides information, support, recognition and training to help those people succeed.
- Concentrates as much on people as on the program.

Since most of us believe in the philosophy of enabling, what many of us need to change is not how we think, but how we do our work. To do that, we need to get a much clearer picture of what enabling looks and feels like, and what's the payoff for changing our leadership behavior

What enabling and mentoring looks and feels like is a very personal thing, because each of us is different. So I'm going to give you a very personal answer to that question by sharing stories about what has enabled me over the years. These are stories of some of the people who have crossed my path and made a real difference in who I am and what I do. They are precious beyond measure! Each of them illustrates different key principles in the enabling/mentoring process.

Principle I:
Enabling means having confidence in a person; seeing potential for growth and helping them to become all they are able to be.

My dad owned a grocery/department store in our small Montana hometown. When I was fifteen, he put me totally in charge of the Christmas window display. When I was sixteen, he turned all buying of teen and young adult clothing over to me. These were significant milestones in developing my confidence and self-esteem.

Ivan Scheier was my first boss in volunteerism. In 1967 he was volunteer pro-tem director of the brand new Volunteer and Information Center in Boulder and I volunteered to be his assistant for six months. I knew nothing about this field, as my previous experience was in human resources for a major corporation. It was Ivan who saw I was a "volunteer-administrator-waiting-to-happen" and talked me into taking the director's position when it became funded and he needed to move on to other dreams. How grateful I am to him for his seeing the possibility in me.

Principle II:

Enabling means being there for a person; sharing your dreams and visions with them.

Harriet Naylor took me under her wing when I was just a bright-eyed, bushy-tailed young pup in this field. Hat spent hours with me, over dinners, in front of our fireplace and long into the night sharing her incredible sense of history and visions of the future for this field. Someone has said, "a vision is a target that beckons," and Hat's vision beckoned me.

Principle III:

Enabling means sharing knowledge and information; helping a person see work as an art, not just a job.

Bill was in charge of the print shop in the first corporation I worked in right out of college. One of my responsibilities was to publish the company newsletter. Bill took me under his wing and lovingly shared his knowledge about paper, type set, color, white space and layout. He taught me that when you love what you do, it isn't work. Twenty years later, I published my own books and drew on every bit of that knowledge he'd so generously shared with me.

Principle IV:

Enabling means loving, trusting and supporting a person; caring enough to give them honest feedback and to hold them accountable.

Harvey, Rich and Lisa are my family. They are the ones who love me, warts and all, and tell me, not always what I want to hear, but what I need to hear. Harvey, my husband, was my most trusted critic. Lisa and Rich, my children, reviewed my calendar when they were home and reminded me it's not how many no's I say but how many yes's that get me in trouble. And they reminded me that I'm the one who's responsible for that.

Principle V:

Enabling means caring about the person as a person, not a role; helping them keep on growing and stretching; celebrating successes and being there in failures.

My colleagues and friends are what make being in this field for almost 40 years a privilege and pure joy.

Left to Right: Marlene's daughter Lisa, husband Harvey, Marlene, son Rich

Principle VI:

An enabler is a mentor who delegates significant responsibility and then helps a person succeed by sharing expertise, information, ideas, knowledge and time.

Jerry was my first boss in the field of human resources. As the personnel manager, he took this blank slate right out of college and in one year turned me into the "Director of Employment and Employee Benefits" for our company. He taught me as fast as I was willing to learn. He sent me to Cal Tech for further training. He heard all my ideas, critiqued them and let me try out the better ones. Jerry stood behind me, let me risk and sometimes fail. When I succeeded, he loved it and he gave me the credit. He was not threatened by my success. I grew by leaps and bounds because that was his intention. He was the best delegator and mentor I've ever seen.

Years later, I worked under an autocratic disabler. It was like being thrown into a tub of ice cold water and not being sure I knew how to swim. I've shared these stories to illustrate that enablers are just ordinary, everyday people. What they share is an attitude about work and people and what's really important in the long run.

There's also a certain bird we can learn from here as well and his name is Jonathan Livingston Seagull.

As the days went past, Jonathan found himself thinking time and again of the Earth, from which he had come. If he had known there just a tenth, just a hundredth of what he knew here, how much more life would have meant! He stood on the sand and fell to wondering if there was a gull back there who might be struggling to break out of his limits, to see the meaning of flight beyond a

*way of travel to get a breadcrumb from a rowboat. Perhaps there might even
have been one made Outcast for speaking his truth in the face of the Flock. And
the more Jonathan practiced his kindness lessons, and the more he worked to
know the nature of love, the more he wanted to go back to Earth. For in spite
of his lonely past, Jonathan Seagull was born to be an instructor, and his own
way of demonstrating love was to give something of the truth that he had seen
to a gull who asked only a chance to see truth for himself.* [2]

That is enabling!

**What is the pay-off for changing our leadership behavior, from doing to
enabling others?**

First, we must recognize and admit the need for change before it makes
any sense to try it. I changed from being a doer to an enabler my second year
as Director of the Volunteer and Information Center. The impetus for change
came when a board member bluntly asked me, "What would happen to this
center if you got hit by a bus tomorrow?" I had to admit honestly, it would
probably have to start over, because no one else knew what I was doing or
how I was doing it. From that point on, I realized that I cared enough about the
Center that I wanted to leave behind me a.) a program that would survive me,
and b.) some enthusiastic, committed and well-trained volunteers and staff
who could carry it to the next step.

What do you want to leave behind *you* when you take a new job or move to
a new city? The need for your program to start all over or a group of enabled
people to carry on? It's an important question!

What I'd like you to take from this is, when it is obvious that many people
are unhappy with the style of leadership being utilized—change it! And that
means really challenging your own behavior, not talking about it or meaning
to but changing it **now.** If you do, here are the pay-offs:

- For subordinates: Robert Townsend, in *Further up the Organization,*
  said, "People who are normally half-dead from boredom and
  frustration during office hours come alive when given a whole job
  and their abilities take a quantum jump. It's better to have champions
  working for you than zombies."[3]

- For clients: They will receive more caring and innovative services
  because people will be able to go beyond coping to dreaming about
  new ways to meet needs, or prevent them. When volunteers and
  staff are using their full potential, clients will be served by fulfilled
  and happy people instead of frustrated and angry workers.

- For the organization: When non-profit and volunteer organizations
  take time to seriously consider what business they are in they can
  move beyond coping and into caring. They will have the human

resources they need (volunteer retention) because volunteers and staff will like working there. And it's easy to recruit people to help in a place that everyone likes.

- For you: Only you can answer that question. I can honestly assure you my greatest accomplishments are not measured in numbers. It's not the hundreds of workshops I've conducted for thousands of people nor all the books I've sold. My most important accomplishments are the times I've had the privilege to be an enabler in someone's life. Opening doors, sharing knowledge at the teachable moment, seeing potential, being there, helping people in large and small ways to become the best they can be.

That, my friend, is what it is all about. And, you have the opportunity to make this real kind of difference in people's lives. You are the ones who understand more about motivation than anyone else, so all you have to do is apply what you already know. You are the ones who can begin to turn your organizations around from disabling people to enabling them, one person at a time and one day at a time. There is an old Chinese proverb: "Hope is like a road in the country; there never was a road, but when many people walk on it, the road comes into existence." That is how change happens.

---

[1] Robert K. Greenleaf, *The Servant as Leader* (Robert K. Greenleaf Center, 1970).
[2] Richard Bach, *Jonathan Livingston Seagull: A Story* (Avon Books, 1970).
[3] Robert Townsend, *Further Up the Organization* (Knopf, 1984).

Motivation:
Placing Right People in Right Jobs

University of Colorado Volunteer Management Certificate Program
Boulder, CO, 1974

I like to think of motivation as a pair of scissors. Scissors have two blades. One blade represents what a person brings to a situation—their talents, gifts and energy. The other blade is what your organization brings to a person. When the two blades come together, motivation happens.

Think about your own organization. A sound volunteer management system in place says to your volunteers that you are committed to utilizing their time and talents well. This is why you do the organizational stuff. It's what you bring to volunteers to equip them for their work. It says that you've done good work and planning, and that you're not going to waste people's time. You're not going to say, "We need you," and then spend half the time figuring out what you need them to do.

Many people view motivation as something you do "to" people. As a leader placing volunteers, it is of vital importance that you understand the link between motivation and matching people to jobs. I like these two quotes that illustrate the connection:

Leaders don't create motivation, they unlock it…They have to help people find the things that are worth committing to…[1]

—John Gardner

Spending time and energy trying to "motivate" people is a waste of effort. The real question is not, "'How do we motivate our people?" If you have the right people on the bus, they will be self-motivated.[2]

—Jim Collins

Now we need to consider the other blade of the scissors—what a person brings to the situation. Both Gardner and Collins point out that motivation comes from within. In the years I've spent placing volunteers and leading groups, it has been extremely helpful to me to try to understand more about the different motivational types of people; what they like to do and don't like to do and therefore what really turns them on (and off).

There is one particular motivational theory that has proven to be invaluable to many of us in the volunteer management profession. It is David McClelland's theory of motivation.[3] When I present this topic in workshops people always respond positively. There is a lot of laughing and head nodding going on. In fact, this topic is one of my most requested workshops. I believe this is because the information is easy for people to relate to and because it has applications far beyond volunteer placement (I will discuss those implications in a little while). It is literally the most important piece of information I've found in helping me understand people. Let me share a bit about it, in hopes that it will help you in both placing and leading your volunteers and staff.

McClelland and his colleague, John W. Atkinson, did their research at Harvard University in the 1950s. McClelland was curious about why one person's favorite job was another's least favorite and why some people liked to figure things out on their own while others wanted clear directions. Starting with the premise that "people spend their time thinking about what motivates them," he and Atkinson conducted extensive studies checking out what people were thinking about while walking, eating, working, studying, even sleeping. What they found was people *do* spend time thinking about what motivates them. They identified three distinct motivational types and labeled them *Achievers, Affiliators* and *Power* (or Influence) people. It is important to point out that one type is not better than the other, but they are different. It is also true that someone can have some traits of each, but one is usually dominant and that's the one that influences motivation.

So let's take a look at the three motivational types and then make some practical applications regarding job placement, meetings and leadership style.

Achievers

Achievers are into accomplishments and results. They like to set goals and solve problems. They want to know where they're heading. They want things to happen in a timely fashion and hate having their time wasted. Achievers are well organized, like deadlines, are moderate risk takers and tend to be articulate. If achievers work under a leader who is poor at delegation, they go crazy. If achievers think they are assigned to a project they can sink their teeth into and then are only given small tasks, their motivation is instantly deflated. In fact, unless they're extremely committed to the cause, you'll lose them.

I can recognize achievers in my workshops because they're the ones sitting at their tables with pencils poised five minutes before the workshop is supposed to start. They like "to-do" lists. You can also identify them by their bulging planners or electronic organizers.

Achievers are often underutilized in membership organizations because so much of the leadership consists of elected positions and committee heads who have served forever. If there is resistance to change, where achievers have no room to grow and stretch themselves, you'll find them coming in one door and going out the other. You can utilize and attract achievers by learning how to use task forces effectively. Search for achievers with good delegation skills and they'll form excellent teams around them.

Everyone knows achievers. Here's Alan's story:

Alan is a business manager who loves to do carpentry in his spare time. The nursery in his small church bothered him. With the exception of a small addition of toys, nothing had been done to fix it up for 20 years. Alan approached members of the church council and they responded with, "yes, let's do that sometime," but nothing ever happened. Finally, Alan took matters into his own hands. He developed a detailed proposal for the council with an exact budget, drawings and pictures of what he envisioned, and a timeline. Instead of asking for the property committee to consider the proposal, he called the church secretary and got himself put on the agenda for the next council meeting. He also called a few members of the council ahead of time and solicited their support.

Alan went into the meeting completely prepared. Since he had done his homework, he anticipated the concerns council members would have and was prepared to address them. He walked out of the meeting with approval for the project and a budget. He recruited members of the church based on their skills to help him with various tasks; a retired electrician to do some rewiring, a carpenter between jobs to help with some framing, women from the sewing group to make new cushions for a window seat. Alan concluded his project with a detailed description of everything he had done and a comparison of his actual and budgeted expenses.

As Alan finished telling me this story he mused, "What if we said to the members of our church, what projects would you like to see accomplished? What if I made myself available to help people see projects through? What exciting things might happen?"

What if? How many volunteers like Alan are there in your organization and how long will they stay?

Affiliators

Affiliators are "people" people. They are sensitive, nurturing and caring. Interaction and being part of a community are what motivates them. For affiliators, the work they're doing is not as important as the people they're doing it with. They are easily hurt, so leaders need to know that affiliators will take more of their time. However, this is time well spent. Affiliators are the people that make an organization a good place to be. They're the ones walking up to new people and striking up a conversation. Affiliators are good barometers of how things are going. If you're wondering how people are feeling about your program, or a certain aspect of it, seek out some affiliators and talk to them.

Affiliators are good persuaders, listeners, and public speakers. They make excellent interviewers, members of listen-care teams or leaders of small groups. They are also great choices for projects like mass mailings. Get a group of affiliators together with a pot of coffee and they'll have the mailing ready before you know it, and they'll have a good time doing it.

A good friend of mine, Jane Justis, told me this story of an affiliator volunteer she had placed while working for Young Life.

We needed a volunteer for some office work and I was involved in the interviewing and placing of a volunteer in our office. Her job was to do data entry in the morning, in a small office outside our reception area. In the afternoon, she switched to the reception area and answered phone calls. Almost immediately, I noticed that in the morning when the volunteer was supposed to be doing data entry, it was almost impossible for her to keep on task. She kept coming out into the reception area to see what was going on. Very little data entry was getting done.

In the afternoons, when she switched to the reception area, she would have lengthy conversations with anyone who called, whether she knew them or not. She was so starved for people contact she was tying up the phone lines. I quickly realized I had put a right person in a wrong job and set out to find her the right job.

She became an assistant volunteer director for half the day and answered the phones for the other half. She loved her jobs and was excellent at them both. She even recruited people while on the phone working as a receptionist. She eventually went on to become an event planner—a job that is perfect for her.

Power People

The word power sometimes has negative connotations, particularly in the volunteer world. We're all "supposed" to be kind and loving towards one another and be working towards the greater good. Power, in the context of McClelland's theory, has both a positive and negative side. There are power-motivated people out there, and our organizations need them, so it's important to understand how they think.

McClelland identified two types of power people whom he categorized as personal and social. Both types of power people like to think about having an impact on people and outcomes. They think long-term and are good strategists. If you want to enact change, you'll need to find some power-motivated people and get them on your side. If you convince them, they'll spend their time thinking about whom they need to influence and how they need to do it.

Personal Power People

It is essential to understand the differences between the two types of power people. Personal power people are into using their power *on* people, usually through manipulation and intimidation. They think in terms of win-lose and, if they perceive someone else is "winning," they instantly think they're losing. They are comfortable with conflict and create a lot of it. I worked for a personal power person for seven years, before I discovered this theory of McClelland's. I was executive director for an agency that was experiencing great success and receiving national attention. And, I was baffled because, the more successful we got, the angrier my boss became. Now I understand that he was threatened by my success. For him power was a finite thing and if I was getting some he thought he was losing some.

These people can be toxic. Knowing that information is power, they may only give you a small piece of what you need to know. If you can think of people who've left your volunteer program "bleeding," there is usually a personal power person involved. These are the people who can also quickly crush programs and new ideas.

Social Power People

Lest you despair, there is a positive side to this. Social power people are the complete opposite. Convince a social power person of your vision and they'll move mountains to see your project happen. Social power people like to influence and impact others in a win-win way. The reason they can do this is because they see power as infinite. The more they give away, the more they get and they aren't threatened by the success of others. Their goal *is* your success. These are the people you need.

Let me share a story about a pastor friend of mine, Warren, who is a social power person.

Warren was called to a parish that had had an affiliator pastor for 15 years. Within the first month he was confronted by two personal power people. One of them was the secretary and the other was the biggest contributor in the congregation. (By the way, social power people are the best at dealing with personal power people because they aren't intimated by them. Never send an affiliator to deal with a personal power person.)

Warren knew he had problems with the secretary because she had set up the files so no one else could get information out of them. Information is power and she knew it. When he realized it he said to her, "We need to redo the filing system and I'd be happy to work with you, just let me know when you'd like to do it. Oh, and we need to get that done in the next three months." Her response was, "No, I've been here for ten years and this is how I do it."

Warren didn't throw a fit, he just replied, "It will be done in three months, let me know if I can help you." At the end of three months nothing had changed. What did Warren do? He fired her. If you're an affiliator say the word out loud now, "fired." The myth was that this secretary was so powerful she'd take half the congregation with her if she left. She did leave, and a few people left, but most people thanked Warren because she had been manipulating and intimidating people in that church for years.

Warren wanted to introduce a new youth program. He presented and got a new program approved by council. Shortly thereafter, a big rancher from the congregation came to him and said, "If you start that program, I'm pulling my money out." Warren looked at him and said, "That would be a shame, but it has been approved and it will begin. You will not hold us hostage with your money." The rancher looked at Warren and said, "But that's worked for years!" The rancher is still a member, still giving his money, still doesn't understand Warren, but he does respect him.

Understand that most people have some characteristics from each motivational type. Interestingly, people's motivational style changes over time and situation. I've been all three. When I was a homemaker, while my children were small, I was an affiliator. When I became a director, I was into achievement. I used to like thinking about program goals, or how shall I write a book or produce a video series. Now I see myself as a social power person. I find myself thinking, how do I influence things that matter? How do I use whatever time and energy I have left to have the most impact on the things I care most about?

If I didn't care passionately about volunteerism I wouldn't do it. When I say I intend to be an influencer, I have a great responsibility to stay in the camp of social power. I have found truth in the concept that the more power I give away the more I get. There's no right order to this. My late husband was moving from being a power/achievement person to becoming more of an affiliator. When you sense a shift in yourself the question to ask yourself is "what do I like to think about now?"

If you'd like to find out what your motivational style is now, use the assessment at the end of this section (pages 52-3). Unfortunately, I don't know the original source, but it's been used in the field for as long as I can remember. It will help you identify your style.

Practical Implications

Interviewing

Once you understand McClelland's theory you will find, when interviewing, that different answers emerge depending on the motivational type of the person you are interviewing. Here's how the different types might respond to the question, "Tell me about your favorite volunteer job in the past?"

- *Achievers* will enthusiastically describe a project or program they **organized**...something new and successful.
- *Affiliators* will often talk about the wonderful group they worked with and will almost always talk about **helping.**
- *Power people* will often relate a long-term **impact** they had, such as a successful building project, getting zoning changed or a great fundraising drive.

Learn to listen to what the person you are interviewing is really trying to tell you about themselves. Watch for when they "light up." This is one of your keys to understanding what motivates your volunteers.

Placement

When you know what motivates your volunteers you can use this knowledge to place them effectively. Here are some questions to help match right people in right jobs.

Will the jobs meet the needs of people with Affiliation needs?

- Is it a team task or will the person work alone?
- How many people does the job require, or does the job allow for regular interaction with others?
- Is there time while doing the job to interact without disturbing other work?
- Can the volunteer develop long-term relationships while doing this job?

Will the job meet the needs of Achievers?

- Will it be clear when the job is done, or is it ongoing and unending? Will success be apparent or can "milestones" be built in?

- Are there clear goals and objectives?
- Does it allow the volunteer to solve problems, decide methods and strategies? Is "figuring it out" part of the job?
- Is there regular feedback?
- Does the job offer independence and challenge?

Will the job meet the needs of Power people?

- Will success result in acclaim, recognition, or other public reward from peers and superiors?
- Does the job present an opportunity to influence others, control work/methods and offer decision-making authority?
- Does the job require working under close supervision? Can it be restructured to offer more independence?
- Does the job have a prestigious title? Does it offer the opportunity to influence outcomes that are important?

Leadership Style

Achievers, Affiliators and Power People have different needs from their leaders. You will be far more successful as a leader if you understand these needs.

- *Achievers* love to work with well-organized, goal-oriented leaders who hold them accountable. They love to be delegated whole projects instead of bits and pieces of projects. They like figuring out how to make it happen.
- *Affiliators* want a leader-friend. They will take more of your time. They appreciate any sort of personal recognition (notes, calls, coffee, etc.). Don't give them work to do alone, they love interaction and groups.
- *Power People* prefer projects where they can influence long-range outcomes and get high visibility.

Meetings

When I train, I'm often seen as a "safe" person. People will tell me things that they won't say to each other, so I'm going to let you know one of the most common reasons volunteers confide to me that they don't volunteer for certain jobs. "The meetings are horrific, they go on forever." You have probably experienced some of these scenarios many times. McClelland's theory helps explain them:

When an Achiever is the leader of a committee:

Her style for running a meeting is to always have an agenda (out ahead of time, with timelines for each item). She starts the meeting on time and it usually lasts about one hour. The purpose of a meeting, for an

Achiever, is to give and get information and make decisions. The other Achievers and Power People love this kind of meeting. However, the Affiliators hate it and usually reconvene their subgroup in the parking lot or on the phone. They say things like, "Can you believe it, Sue never even got a chance to talk?" "He cut me off and I hadn't even begun to tell everyone about my horrible day." "We need a meeting without a silly time limit where everyone can say their piece."

When an Affiliator is the leader of a committee:

His style is to have no agenda; you build it as you go. Meetings don't start until everyone has arrived and had a chance to do a personal check-in. There is a lot of discussion that frequently goes off-topic. Usually there is coffee or a meal. The other Affiliators are delighted, as they believe meetings are an opportunity to build relationships and do a little business. The meeting lasts "as long as it takes." Needless to say, the Achievers are climbing the wall and the Power People have left.

When a Power Person is leader of a committee:

Personal power: this person is almost always an autocrat, very controlling and intimidating. The agenda is set by him/her and very little if any time is allowed for discussion. Most often the committee is used to rubber stamp what the leader has decided and he/she takes credit for anything accomplished.

Social power: This leader is the ultimate enabler and collaborative decision maker. Input from all members is sought and everyone is encouraged to participate. He/she makes an effort to determine the strengths of each committee member and delegates the work to be done accordingly. The committee becomes a synergistic team.

What I've learned to do is modify my style of leadership to acknowledge and respect some of the needs of all three groups instead of the needs of only one. Remember, effective groups need all three styles, as each brings different strengths to the group. Here's an example of how I would structure a meeting that takes place right after work:

I would prepare and distribute an agenda. The meeting would include a simple soup/sandwich meal. The first half hour would be for eating and socializing—no business. The meeting starts on time and follows the agenda, but I build in a little more time for discussion than I predicted would be necessary. I adjourn the meeting on time, but leave the coffee pot on for those who want to stay and socialize. The goal is to meet some of the needs of everyone and not all of the needs of one motivational type.

This problem of meetings and addressing the needs of Affiliators and Achiever/Power People is universal. I recently had a call to my office from a woman who represented a group of Middle-Eastern women who wanted to become more involved in their community. She said, "Do you have anything that will help us with meetings? We are driving each other crazy. Those of us raised in the U.S., who are working, come to meetings and want to get things done. The women who have recently arrived and the older women are upset with us. They think we are cold. They want to spend two hours socializing and then think about business." I told her I had just the thing for her, and sent her the information I've just shared with you.

My friend Arlene Schindler is an incredibly effective woman who has a long and impressive resume in public service. She was associate Peace Corps director in Africa, served as vice president of Prison Fellowship and was director of volunteer services for Special Olympics International. As you may have guessed, Arlene is an Achiever/Social Power Person. At one time she had an Affiliator for a secretary. Arlene traveled extensively, so each time she returned to her office from a trip, her main goal was to get in the office, check her messages, go through the mail and get things organized. What was Arlene's secretary's goal? To get caught up, look at pictures, find out how things were going. Arlene and her secretary were driving each other crazy.

Finally, Arlene came up with a plan designed to meet both their needs. When she returned from a trip, Arlene would go into the office an hour before her secretary was due to arrive. She'd get through the messages and mail. When her secretary came in, Arlene would get up, pour a cup of coffee, go to her secretary's desk, sit down and chat for 15 minutes. They got caught up and, because Arlene was not in her office, she could control the length of time away from her desk. By being aware, attentive and intentional Arlene made sure both their needs were met.

Phone calls

As a leader, you also need to vary your style on the telephone to fit the volunteer you're calling.

- **Achievers** and **Power People** like short, concise, precise phone calls—friendly but business-like.
- **Affiliators** like the leader-friend who is interested in catching up on what's new in their life and cares about them and their family. Some chit-chat is important. The information/business is secondary to the personal connections.

In meetings and phone calls, you can see how easy it is when dealing with the same type as you are—but the challenge is not to de-motivate those who are different.

E-mails [section added in the 1990s]

E-mail has made many a volunteer director's life easier. One message, a distribution list and the flick of a button and you've notified everyone at once—Achievers and Power People love it. If you are an Achiever or a Power Person sending out e-mails, be sure and include a brief sentence or two that makes the message a little more personal. This will appeal to the Affiliators of your group.

You may find Affiliators doing the same thing via e-mail that they do on the phone. They send out a message with an inspirational quote, or attach a picture, or funny story, fill you in on what's going on and then at the bottom of the message comes, "Oops, almost forgot, the meeting has been changed to such-and-so date and such-and-so time."

Since Affiliators crave people contact, you may find that these are also the people who don't regularly check their e-mail. If you are a leader of a group, be sure and verify with all the members how they would like to be contacted as some still do prefer the phone call.

Training

You are probably getting the idea by now that deeper understanding of the motivational types has implications in almost all areas of volunteer management. Setting up trainings is somewhat like setting up meetings.

- **Achievers** and **Power People** are looking for content. They will tolerate group experiences but what they are saying to themselves is, "I did not come here to share my ignorance with somebody else." They get nervous if you hold hands too long.
- **Affiliators** start off by wanting name tags so everybody knows everybody else. They want a group building experience while the Achievers are thinking, "I belong already, what are we going to *do*?" Affiliators also like doing exercises and breaking off into small discussion groups.

When I train, I always create sessions that alternate between content and small group interaction. This way I meet some of the needs of everyone. The principle holds true for any group you work with.

Teams/Task Forces/Committees

As I said before, all groups need all three types of motivational types to function well. You need to think carefully when you think of the people you want to place on your task force or committee. If you're trying to bring about significant change, look for a Social Power Person. Try to avoid a Personal Power Person unless it is absolutely essential. Then do it deliberately, fully aware that you will make sacrifices to achieve your greater goal.

For task forces that aren't "rocking the boat," look for Achievers with the ability to delegate. Affiliators give you a barometer of what's going on in the group. Although Achievers and Affiliators have very different styles, sometimes a combination of the two, as co-leaders, makes for a highly dynamic, effective task force. The Achiever does the organizing piece of the project while the Affiliator is out pitching the cause, interviewing, recruiting and attracting people to the vision and the group. The following is a true story of a team project at a church. Now that you understand a little about the motivational types, see if you can identify what went wrong.

> One Sunday our pastor made an announcement that the church council had decided to embark on a project to make personal contact with every member of our church. This was an ambitious idea because our church had over 1000 members. Our pastor, a real people person, enthusiastically explained that on a certain Sunday afternoon, teams would be stopping by at member's houses to deliver a loaf of bread and to spend a little time chatting about how the members thought things were going at church. My husband and I were impressed with the idea and looked forward to talking with the team. We had lots of ideas and were eager to become more deeply involved.

> On the appointed Sunday, we unfortunately missed the team visit, but were pleased to find a loaf of bread on our doorstep. At our small group Bible study that week, though, we started hearing complaints. One couple, long-time members of the church told our group that no one visited them. When they asked why, they were told, "Well, it turned out we didn't have enough teams to reach everybody and so we decided not to visit the long-standing members." This decision, unfortunately, was not announced in advance and caused hurt feelings among the long-time members.

> We were interested in learning about the feedback the church council got so after a month my husband asked one of the council members about the visiting project and what they'd found out. He said, "The purpose of the visit was to make people feel good about our church and let them tell the teams what they thought. But we didn't gather any official 'feedback'; we just wanted to let people talk." Many members who spoke with the visiting teams were aghast when they learned this. Several were heard making comments like, "that was a waste of time," and "I can't believe they went to all that work and came away with nothing."

Can you see what went wrong here? My guess is that the pastor and council members planning this event were Affiliators. They were interested in making contact and relating to people. They wanted the church members to feel valued and appreciated. The Achievers and Power People in the congregation didn't see it this way. They felt that all that work and effort was a waste of time because it was all relational. Achievers would have preferred questionnaires or forms to fill out so that there could be a gathering of information. They wanted to see results, new goals, objectives and plans. This story truly illustrates why it is critical to involve a variety of motivational types on your committees.

Finally, let me encourage you to share this information about motivational style with your staff, volunteers and interviewers. Retaining good volunteers is a high priority and continuing concern of all organizations I work with and proper volunteer placement significantly increases the odds of a volunteer remaining committed to your organization. A good understanding of styles and proper placement of people in jobs can prevent a host of other personnel problems as well. Sharpen your own skills in identifying motivational types.

Helping your staff and leaders understand the motivational power of being treated as valuable, valued members is incredibly important. When we get our hearts right around volunteers and get management systems in place, and then get creative about putting out our invitation, and thoughtfully think about placing them to enhance their talents, interests and energy, I truly believe there are plenty of volunteers out there, willing and able to help us do anything we need done.

---

[1] John Gardener, *On Leadership* (The Free Press, 1990), 14.

[2] Jim Collins, *Good to Great* (Harper Business, 2001), 74.

[3] D. C. McClelland, *The Achieving Society* (Van Nostrand, 1961).

Motivational Analysis
(original source unknown)

Each of the following questions has three choices. Chose the one in each question that most closely fits your own motivations. Remember, there are no wrong answers. Place an "X" before the letter of your choice.

1. _____ a.   When doing a job, I seek feedback.
   _____ b.   I prefer to work alone and am eager to be my own boss.
   _____ c.   I seem to be uncomfortable when forced to work alone.

2. _____ a.   I go out of my way to make friends with new people.
   _____ b.   I enjoy a good argument.
   _____ c.   After starting a task, I am not comfortable until it is completed.

3. _____ a.   Status symbols are important to me.
   _____ b.   I am always getting involved in group projects.
   _____ c.   I work better when there is a deadline.

4. _____ a.   I work best when there is some challenge involved.
   _____ b.   I would rather give orders than take them.
   _____ c.   I am sensitive to others - especially when they are mad.

5. _____ a.   I am eager to be my own boss.
   _____ b.   I accept responsibility eagerly.
   _____ c.   I try to get personally involved with my superiors.

6. _____ a.   I am uncomfortable when forced to work alone.
   _____ b.   I prefer being my own boss, even when others feel a joint effort is required.
   _____ c.   When given responsibility, I set measurable standards of high performance.

7. _____ a.   I am very concerned about my reputation or position.
   _____ b.   I have a desire to out-perform others.
   _____ c.   I am concerned with being liked and accepted.

8. _____ a.   I enjoy and seek warm, friendly relationships.
   _____ b.   I attempt complete involvement in a project.
   _____ c.   I want my ideas to predominate.

9. _____ a.   I desire unique accomplishments.
   _____ b.   It concerns me when I am being separated from others.
   _____ c.   I have a need and desire to influence others.

10. _____ a.   I think about consoling and helping others.
    _____ b.   I am verbally fluent.
    _____ c.   I am restless and innovative.

11. _____ a.   I set goals and think about how to attain them.
    _____ b.   I think about ways to change people
    _____ c.   I think a lot about my feelings and the feelings of others.

Motivational Analysis Key

1. a.   Achievement
   b.   Influence
   c.   Affiliation

2. a.   Affiliation
   b.   Influence
   c.   Achievement

3. a.   Influence
   b.   Affiliation
   c.   Achievement

4. a.   Achievement
   b.   Influence
   c.   Affiliation

5. a.   Influence
   b.   Achievement
   c.   Affiliation

6. a.   Affiliation
   b.   Influence
   c.   Achievement

7. a.   Influence
   b.   Achievement
   c.   Affiliation

8. a.   Affiliation
   b.   Achievement
   c.   Influence

9. a.   Achievement
   b.   Affiliation
   c.   Influence

10. a.   Affiliation
    b.   Influence
    c.   Achievement

11. a.   Achievement
    b.   Influence
    c.   Affiliation

Influencing Outcomes You Care About

University of Colorado Volunteer Management Certificate Program
Boulder, CO, 1981

I believe the transforming movement that raises the quality of any institution, large or small, begins with the initiative of one individual person—no matter how large the institution or how substantial the movement.

—John Gardner

Which outcomes should we try to influence? We need to choose our battles, so I would prioritize outcomes by these criteria:

- Those we care deeply about—personally and professionally.
- Those that influence the quality and effectiveness of volunteer involvement in a changing organizational environment as opposed to "saving our jobs."
- Those that help realize our dreams and visions for a better quality of life for our clients, our communities and our world.

As you understand more about motivation and power (see previous presentation, "Motivation: Placing Right People in Right Jobs"), you can develop your strategy for influencing people with the need for power. Write a profile of the key person you want to influence. Include everything you know about that person including:

- Known likes and dislikes
- The accomplishments that make them most proud
- Their motivational style

Based on their motivational style, identify their needs, interests and concerns regarding the proposal you are bringing them. Use all this information and the tips I've shared on motivation to develop your persuasion strategy.

I'd also like to share an alternative method (remember, there's always more than one way to do something) for developing a strategy. The following are questions that should be answered when planning how to achieve a goal that requires influencing others (define clearly and concisely):

Influence - Achievement Worksheet
1. What outcome would you like to see occur?
2. Who must be influenced to have the desired outcome occur?
3. What is your source of influence (power) with the person(s) identified above?
4. What will the person(s) do if you have been successful in your attempt to influence?
5. What is your strategy for influencing the person(s) to work toward the desired outcome?
6. What action must occur to achieve the desired outcome? By whom?
7. If the desired outcome occurs, what is the "pay off" to you? ...to the person(s) you're attempting to influence? ...to others?
8. If the desired outcome fails to occur, what happens to you? ...to the person(s) you're attempting to influence? ...to others?
9. What obstacles, real and potential, must be overcome? (Consider obstacles in influencing others along with obstacles to achieving the desired outcome.)
10. What can be done to avert or minimize the obstacles?
11. How intensely do you want the desired outcome to occur?

Finally, as you build your strategy you should be aware of potential conflicts and be prepared to address them. These are the common levels of conflict:

-   *Data:* Questions that come up about how you gathered your data or decided to interpret it or requests for more data.
-   *Process:* Questions about the process you've used.
-   *Goals:* Questions about your goals; are they the right ones?
-   *Values:* Questions about your core beliefs.

Each level gets more difficult to manage. It's relatively easy to change data or get more information but if your values are light years apart that will be tough to reconcile.

Steps to Influential Problem Solving
There are basically three steps to creative and effective problem solving:

1. **Clearly and creatively determine the problem you want to solve.** The goal you want to achieve, what you want to have happen. Then, we'll learn how to explore as many alternatives as possible and be sure it's the real problem and not a symptom.

2. **Strategize how to make it happen.** That is simply thoughtfully thinking through ahead of time the vital questions about the *who, how, what* and *when* of influencing outcomes. As P.T. Barnum said, "You can't sell the peanuts if you can't get 'em in the tent!"

3. **Negotiate with whoever can say "yes" or "no" to this idea.** And, doing it in such a way that you get a "yes" (at least most of the time).

Step 1: Clearly and Creatively Defining the Problem and Your Goal in Solving It.

The most helpful tool I've found to do this is one that helps you turn a gripe into a goal. The "Gripe to Goal" exercise below helps you identify your real problem. Try it!

This is such a critical, yet often neglected, first step. How often have you had a bright idea and gone rushing into your boss the minute he or she hit the office, or caught them in the hall and sprung it on them? This is usually deadly if you are really trying to influence an outcome you care about. The boss, supervisor or board isn't ready, but neither are you. The idea very likely died because it deserved to.

How to Help a Person Identify the Problem
Gripe to Goal Exercise

Step 1. My gripe (or frustration or anxiety) is _____

_____

_____

Step 2. My real concern is _____

_____

_____

Step 3. *Turn your concern into a wish by completing this sentence:*
What I'm really wishing for is _____

_____

_____

Step 4. Therefore, my goal is to _____

_____

_____

Step 5. Who can say "yes" or "no" to this goal (name the person)?

_____

Step 2: Strategize How to Make It Happen

Let me define how I'm using the word strategize here: Strategizing is thoughtfully thinking through ahead of time *who*, *how* and *when* you will take your ideas to others.

This is where the skills of influence become extremely important and to become an influencer you need to understand some ideas about power. The word "power" comes from the Latin word "to be able." Let's start with two definitions of power:

- The ability to influence/impact people and situations.
- The ability to cause or prevent change.

Go back to your "Gripe to Goal" exercise. The last question on the list asks "Who can say 'yes' or 'no' to this request?" Always remember, you influence persons, not groups. As you begin to strategize how to make your goal happen, there may be a group or board you wrote down as an answer to this question. Within groups, there are always people that have more power or influence than others do. You need to identify those individuals and your strategy should focus on influencing them.

Step 3: Negotiating with Whoever Can Say "Yes" or "No" to this Idea.

You've creatively identified your problem and solution and you've developed a strategy and considered potential conflicts. Now it's time to learn some negotiation skills. Good influencers are good negotiators, and it's simply a matter of developing your skills. The goals of negotiation are to:

1. Create wise agreements…
2. that are efficiently arrived at, and…
3. improve relationships.

Abraham Lincoln once said, "When I'm getting ready to reason with someone, I spend one-third of my time thinking about what I'm going to say and two-thirds of my time thinking about what he's going to say."

I have negotiated for many things that I've cared about during my career in volunteerism. Here are some tips for negotiation:

- Carefully select the person(s) who will be your spokesperson. Again, I encourage you to read the presentation on Motivation. This may be your cause but you may not be the best person to present your proposal. If you are an affiliator and the person you need to influence is a personal power person, you are doomed to failure. Influence an influencer (in this case preferably a social power person) to be your spokesperson.

- Be conscious of the importance of timing. Almost no new idea will look good in the midst of an audit, grant deadline or annual meeting.
- Always recheck your assumptions as you move through the process.
- Time and patience are power. Don't be forced into unwanted or unwise deadlines.
- Understand the sources of power and understand their unique needs (for both yourself and the person you are trying to influence).
- Clarify the outcomes you want and be specific.
- Avoid "take-it-or-leave-it" tactics.
- Dare to take a risk.
- You don't need to be loved by everyone!
- Do your homework.
- Examine **all** alternatives.
- Be a bit unpredictable.
- Have high aspirations. Ask for what you really need, not just what you think you can get.

I'd like to share a true story that illustrates the importance of negotiating. One of my students in a weeklong creative problem-solving course at the University of Colorado was a volunteer coordinator at a large hospital in North Dakota. When I asked each of my students what problem they wanted to work on that week, Yvonne said, "I want to be able to serve hamburgers at the hospital recognition picnic next summer."

I told her, if that's all she needed, we could call the administrator of the hospital and request it. (I was pretty sure that serving hamburgers must be a symptom of a bigger problem.) Yvonne then told me that every July all the hospital department managers served hamburgers to the rest of the staff and volunteers, but she felt she was always on the wrong side of the grill. A-ha! The real problem emerged. Yvonne wanted to be a department manager with the status and salary that went with it. Now that was a problem worth working on. Throughout the weeklong class, we worked on all three of the steps and a few months later I got a postcard from Yvonne. It said, "This is to inform you that I strategized and DID IT! I'll be joining the ranks of the hamburger fryers at the next hospital picnic." She signed the note: "The Newest Department Manager."

Enhancing Our
Creative Problem-Solving Skills

University of Colorado Volunteer Management Certificate Program
Boulder, CO, 1981

Do you recall the movie, *Dead Poet's Society*, with Robin Williams? In the film, he plays a teacher in an exclusive boy's school and uses creative and unusual ways of teaching English literature. This causes conflict with the headmaster. In one scene, they are arguing and the headmaster states the purpose of education is "to pass on tradition, develop discipline and get the boys into good colleges." Williams' character vehemently disagrees and says the purpose of education is "to help the boys think for themselves." If you've seen the film you'll recall some of the wonderful words of wisdom the teacher imparts to the boys:

- *Carpe diem*—Seize the day.

- "Make something extraordinary of your life."

- "All of life is a poem—perhaps you will add a line."

Unfortunately, far too many organizations seem to agree with the fictional school's headmaster. They not only don't encourage creativity, they barely tolerate it. Many people let their creative juices dry up, especially in times of crisis and great change, which is just when they need it most.

I'd like to share this allegory with you:

Once upon a time there was a land where the whole community lived under one big glass dome. For generations the families had been born, lived and died under the glass dome. And, the story that passed down from generation to generation was, if you ever DID step outside of the glass dome, you would surely die. So no one had ever dared to step outside the glass dome.

In fact, the community had decided that there was one crime so dastardly that the punishment for anyone who committed that crime would be to banish him outside the dome, which would be certain death for him.

No one, but no one, had ever committed that crime. Then one day, to the community's horror, one man did commit such a crime.

The punishment was swift. The whole community escorted the man to the edge of the glass dome and pushed him out into the world beyond. Then they all pressed their noses to the wall of the glass dome to watch the man die.

At first the man laid on the ground, face down, shivering with fear. His muscles were clenched up as he braced himself for what would certainly happen.

But nothing happened. After a bit, he rolled over and looked around and seeing nothing threatening in sight he ventured to sit up and look around. As the people in the glass dome watched intently, the man slowly stood up. Then, to their amazement the man began to dance softly in the green, green grass, moving this way and that, trying out his arms and legs that seemed to work perfectly well.

Then he began to jump up and down and to shout joyously and to beckon to the people under the dome to COME ON OUT AND DANCE WITH ME! The people were filled with confusion and bewilderment to see this happy man dancing when they had expected to see him die a horrible death. The confusion and stress grew so great within them they finally had to take action. They got buckets of black paint and painted the walls of the dome black as high as they could reach so they could no longer see the dancing man. Then they all breathed a sigh of relief and went back to just the way things had been before that day.

What was the crime the man had committed? He was an innovator.

Each time I read this allegory I find myself reacting in a real and personal sense. It is so reminiscent of situations I have experienced and witnessed in organizations. It vividly illustrates a phenomenon that I feel contributes heavily to turnover in organizations. I call this phenomenon *turnout* (not to be confused with a much more frequently discussed cause of turnover, burnout).

Creative problem-solving skills are essential in our changing world. This is an area of study that has always fascinated me. Everyone needs new solutions and we, as volunteer managers, must be able to offer them in our area of expertise. Never underestimate the difference one person can make and it just possibly might be you!

Understanding and Embracing Creativity

Let's start with some definitions:

Create: to evolve from one's own thought or imagination.

Innovate: to bring in something new—make changes in anything established. (Organizations and people resist change— it's human nature.)

Artist and psychoanalyst Desy Safan-Gerard said, "Everyone looking for answers to problems is engaged in creative work—whether the end result is a painting, a report or a reorganization plan. Creativity occurs when there is successful communication between a person and their work." Let me give some suggestions for building a creative environment in your organization.

Keep It Natural

Keep it as natural as possible—as few rules/policies as you can.

In Robert Townsend's classic, *Up the Organization*, he tells the story of when he became the CEO of Avis Rent-a-Car when the company was almost bankrupt. The board of directors told him to fire the whole top management team, but Townsend wanted to work with the team before making a decision. He ended up only letting one person go. What Townsend did do was change the way people worked at Avis. He created a position called "Vice President in Charge of Killing Things" to help managers get rid of all the old tasks that took enormous amounts of time and accomplished nothing.[1]

A popular model of learning that I like very much describes four levels of competence:

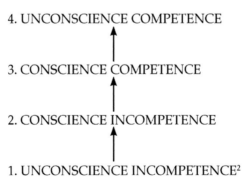

4. UNCONSCIENCE COMPETENCE

3. CONSCIENCE COMPETENCE

2. CONSCIENCE INCOMPETENCE

1. UNCONSCIENCE INCOMPETENCE[2]

Every new person starts in a company at #1. The goal is to move through the stages with training and education to get to #4. That level is where the real challenge lies because you've stopped growing. You need to delegate some of what you do well, so you can take on a new challenge and keep the learning cycle growing.

There are some important implications here for volunteer managers:

- Don't sanction or ignore incompetence. The real enemy of the best is not the worst, but the good enough.

- Give people the right to risk and give them second and third chances.

- Teach people not to be incompetent. Hold volunteers accountable and never lower standards—it's the ultimate put down.

- People can learn to be creative.

Blocks to Creativity

There are so many ways that we block our own creativity. We often aren't even aware of them. Here are some common blocks that I compiled after reading multiple books on creativity while researching my second book, *Survival Skills for Managers*. On the next page are some common blocks. Do you recognize yourself in any of these? If so, acknowledge them and find ways to overcome them.

Unblocking Creativity

Question Like Children

Neil Postman said, "Children enter school as question marks and leave as periods."[3] And, I would add, far too many stay "periods" the rest of their lives. The challenge for us in creative problem solving is how to turn back into questions marks—and possibly even an exclamation point (or, as my kids called them, "excitement marks").

Researchers tell us that the most creative people in the world are kids under five. (They score an average of 95% on creativity tests. Adults taking the same tests score an average of 2%.) This fact brings to mind a concept from Abraham Maslow:

> *Give an adult a hammer and he'll treat the whole world like a nail. Give a child a hammer and they may dig with it, sculpt with it, weigh down papers with leaves in between or knock down apples with it…because nobody told them it was to hit a nail with.*[4]

Think of the characteristics and traits of kids under five. They are:

- Curious
- Energetic
- Determined
- Fearless
- Playful

Block	Characteristics
Fear of Failure	Won't take risks; settle for less in order to avoid possible pain or shame from failing.
Reluctance to Play	Literal, serious problem-solving style. No "playing around." Fear of seeming foolish or silly.
Resource Myopia	Failure to see one's own strengths. Lack of appreciation for resources within one's environment.
Frustration Avoidance	Giving up too soon when faced with an obstacle. Avoids pain or discomfort associated with change or novel solutions.
Custom-Bound	Emphasis on traditional ways of doing things; too much reverence for the past; tendency to conform.
Impoverished Fantasy Life	Mistrusts, ignores or demeans inner images and visualization of self and others; over-values the "objective"; lacks imagination in the sense of "let's pretend" or "what if?"
Fear of the Unknown	Avoidance of situations that lack clarity or have an unknown chance of succeeding; a need to know the future before proceeding.
Need for Balance	Inability to tolerate disorder, confusion or ambiguity. Excessive need for balance, order and symmetry.
Reluctance to Exert Influence	Fear of seeming too aggressive or pushy. Ineffective in making oneself heard.
Impoverished Emotional Life	Fails to appreciate the motivational power of emotion. Lacks awareness of importance of feelings in achieving commitment to individual and group efforts.
Unintegrated Ying-Yang	Polarizes issues into opposites rather than knowing how to integrate the best of both sides.
Sensory Dullness	Poor sensitivity, atrophy of capacities, doesn't use senses as a way of knowing.

The characteristic I remember best about my children at that age is the incessant, never-ending questions: *"why? why? why not?"* If we want to be creative problem solvers, we've got to re-learn how to do this. The real trick however, is not just to ask questions, but to ask the right questions. Anthony Jay was quoted saying, "A non-creative mind can spot wrong answers but it takes a creative mind to spot wrong questions."

It's been my observation during the last decade, that a great many organizations, agencies and churches are operating programs and systems that worked once upon a time. But, they somehow have failed to note that the whole world has changed around them, including the needs and realities of the people they serve. They just "keep on keeping on" whether what they're doing works or not. Could it be the leaders are periods instead of questions marks? And when budgets get cut and needs increase (a situation we all know about) the automatic response seems to be to work harder and harder and longer and longer and faster and faster until they eventually burn out from the process.

If there is any time for training, it's almost always used for building skills to help us do things right (and thus become more efficient) instead of sessions exploring how to do the right thing (which would help us become more effective). Who's got time for questions in a situation like this?

Creativity expert, Edward de Bono, calls this the difference between vertical and lateral thinking.[5] A vertical thinker just keeps digging a hole deeper, hoping eventually it will work. A lateral thinker will try digging in another place, and another and another, until he finds the right hole. The key difference is in our attitude about alternatives. Without exploring alternatives, we inevitably get in ruts both in our personal lives and at work. Someone once observed, "The only difference between a rut and a grave is how deep it is."

Imagine Like Children

Another trait that kids have that we need to recapture is imagination. My son, Rich, has always had a vivid imagination. Between the ages of four and five, he had an imaginary friend named George. One day I watched as Rich showed George around an elaborate Lego® block village he'd created. He pointed to one building and said, "And this is the Standard station that Jesus visited in 1938."

George was so real to Rich that we had to leave room for him in the car and set a place for him at the table. We were a bit worried about how we'd handle it when Rich went to school, but Rich took care of the problem himself. A few months before he was to start school, we were going on a car trip. All of a sudden, Rich piped up from the back seat and announced that George was not with us because he had moved to Alaska and got married. (We never heard about George again.)

How can we hope to change the world or even a wee small corner of it unless we can clearly and vividly imagine it the way we'd like it to be? Albert Einstein said, "Imagination is more important than knowledge, for knowledge is limited to all we know and understand while imagination embraces the entire world (and all there ever will be to know and understand)."[6]

So, our challenge in a session on creative problem solving and influencing outcomes is to explore as many ways as we can to jar loose the creativity bottled inside of every one of us, and to have fun doing it! I'm talking about becoming change agents—and we can learn how to do that. It takes skill, practice and a passionate caring.

We need to understand much more about the process of creative problem solving and then we can move on to the whole business of understanding and utilizing power and influence to help get those ideas accepted and implemented. This is the hard part: we must realize all the good ideas in the world won't make any difference unless they're implemented.

Key Roles to Play

There are four important roles we must learn to play in this idea-making process if we are to be truly creative. Each is essential but different.[7]

1. Explorer   3. Judge
2. Artist   4. Warrior

1. **The Explorer:** Here you are searching for new information, data, experiences and ideas to process, finding the "raw materials" to work with. This is how you're able to come up with alternatives, which are crucial. Someone once observed, "There's nothing more dangerous than a person with an idea— if it's the only idea they have!" How do you get new information to process? This is a very important question. One strategy is to try doing something new yourself. I have personally found that when I've tried new things, visited new places, it opens up my mind to new possibilities about my work. What new thing have you done lately? Think of:

- hobbies
- travel
- reading
- people
- trying new things, foods, classes

I've recently tried snorkeling, parasailing, international travel and river rafting—all of which have given me new insights in my work life.

2. **The Artist:** As the artist, you are turning your information and resources into new ideas—making them your own. This is your right brain work. Let me share a couple of examples.

The story of Velcro®
We've all used Velcro, that miraculous invention that helps us close jackets, gloves, etc. The idea was born when the inventor went for a hike and came home to find burrs stuck all over his woolen socks. He was fascinated by how they stuck together and experimented until he could re-create a similar product.

The story of Post-its®
Who doesn't use Post-its, at home, at the office, a dozen times a day? The idea for this wonderful product came from a 3M employee who sang in a choir and got frustrated that the paper bookmarks he put in his hymnbook each Sunday kept falling out. Wouldn't it be great to be able to have a marker that stuck but wouldn't tear the pages when removed? So he put out the challenge to his co-workers at 3M and

someone remembered they'd made a batch of glue that didn't stick very well. A need + an idea + creativity = a new solution.

3. **The Judge:** Here you evaluate the merits of the idea. It's your left brain work. Unfortunately, not all ideas are winners and it's helpful if we find that out ourselves. You need to stand back and objectively look at your glorious, one-of-a-kind masterpiece the "artist" created and analyze what needs to be added, deleted, changed, rearranged or even discarded. Only after completing these three steps are you ready to move on to trying to make it happen. And then you become...

4. **The Warrior (the influencer!):** Now it's time to carry your idea into action. This is where the faint-hearted fall by the wayside because bringing in something new means something else must die so you're in for a battle. As you evaluate your plan and prepare it for presentation remember what I like to call the 3 S's:

- the System
- the Status quo
- the Stinkers

When I entered this field I was the first director of the first volunteer center in the state of Colorado, and one thing I enjoyed most was developing new and needed services (youth and senior volunteer programs). Many of these programs went very well, but a few failed and I never liked that. My late husband, Harvey, shared a wonderful saying with me that helped me stay a risk-taker, in spite of disappointment:: "You cannot be creative if you don't dare risk; you cannot risk if you don't dare fail; it is not failure if you learn from it."

---

[1] Townsend, Robert. *Up the Organization.* (Alfred A. Knopf, 1970).

[2] I could not find a specific source for the Levels of Competence, but many references exist for it in educational theory literature. Walt Disney also promoted this idea. For more details, see http://www.businessballs.com/consciouscompetencelearningmodel.htm.

[3] Neil Postman and Charles Weingartner, *Teaching as a Subversive Activity* (Delta, 1971).

[4] Maslow's Hammer concept has been stated and paraphrased many times over throughout his works. http://www.abraham-maslow.com/m_motivation/Maslows_Hammer.asp. This version is how I recollect it.

[5] Edward De Bono, *Lateral Thinking: Creativity Step by Step* (Harper & Row, 1970).

[6] Ashton Applewhite and Tripp Evans eds., *And I Quote* (St. Martin's Press, 1992), 157.

[7] Roger von Oech, *A Kick in the Seat of the Pants* (Harper & Row, 1985), 11.

Polishing the Potential of Volunteer and Staff Teams

International Conference on Volunteer Administration
Little Rock, AR, October 1993

I am delighted to be able to discuss with all of you what I consider to be the #1 challenge in the field of volunteerism today—the relationship between volunteers and paid staff. The fascinating thing is, I could have said this same thing 20 years ago and it would have been just as true. I believe it is time for our field to stop wringing our hands and wallowing in the "ain't it awfuls" about this issue and get on with some clear, positive solutions.

I want to share some useful insights and tools to begin the process of polishing the potential of effective and creative volunteer/staff teams. To do this, I will discuss three major topics:

- Definitions and types of teams
- Understanding the problem
- My eight steps to effective volunteer/staff team building

Definitions/Types of Teams

The dictionary tells us a team is any group organized to work together. That sounds so simple—why is it so hard?

William Dyer in his book, *Team Building : Proven Strategies for Improving Team Performance*, goes a bit further: "Teams are collections of people who must rely on group collaboration if each member is to experience the optimum of success and goal achievement."[1] A-ha! Perhaps the key is the word *collaboration*.

Then there is *Roget's Thesaurus* which adds this colorful alternative: "two or more draft animals harnessed together"—not totally unlike the image of some volunteer/staff teams I've seen.

Obviously, we have all experienced many types of teams. Perhaps the most helpful model I've run across to help diagnose not only what a team is presently like, but also to suggest what it might become, is one drawn from the scientific theories of biology. Three types of teams found by biologists are:

Parasitic
Symbiotic
Synergistic

Parasitic teams: These are *competitive,* representated by the formula $1 + 1 = <2$. In such teams, the issue of turf dominates everything. Staff sees volunteers as interlopers and competitors so the energy of the "team" tends to go toward turf protection and conflicts instead of concentrating on the mission. (These kinds of teams can also be made up of all paid staff defending their departments or all volunteers where the old leadership protects their turf from new volunteers). There are an appalling number of interagency parasitic team efforts.

Basically, the experience that this type of team produces is "we all got out less than we put in" and it is a frustrating, unrewarding waste of time and energy.

This, my friends, has been the root of many of the problems surrounding volunteer/staff relationships, and it must stop! It is obscene to waste our precious and scarce human resources like this in a world that has increasing unmet human needs.

Symbiotic teams are *cooperative,* represented as $1 + 1 = 2$. Such volunteer and staff teams have been the goal of our field for the past 10 or 15 years. This is why we have developed sound and effective volunteer management tools and techniques (job descriptions, interviewing, training) so we could have a fair exchange of value-for-value between the volunteer's needs, abilities and motives and the organizational, staff, and client's needs.

Synergistic teams: These are *collaborative,* represented as $1 + 1 = 4$. Where good volunteer administration is practiced, the shift from parasitic to symbiotic teamwork is evident and should be celebrated. However, the challenge before us in this time of dramatic increases in needs and ever-shrinking resources is to learn the invaluable skill of synergistic team building, in which, through collaboration of volunteers and staff, $1 + 1$ can equal **4.** In other words, we can all get out of the experience more than any one puts in (or, we are better together than alone). In the process, the client is better served than ever before, and neither staff nor volunteers burn out in the process.

I know, it sounds impossible but it isn't. And, when we learn to do it, our field will be on the cutting edge of what is needed by all organizations. Are we up to the challenge?

Perhaps one of the most significant books on leadership and management I have ever read is a small paperback called *Leadership Is an Art* by Max DePree. It should be required reading for anyone truly committed to forming synergistic teams. DePree says, "The needs of the team are best met when we meet the needs of individual persons. By conceiving a vision and pursuing it together, we can solve our problems of effectiveness and productivity! And we may at the same time fundamentally alter the concept of work."[2]

What that says to me is that we must truly care about the needs and concerns of paid staff as well as those of the volunteers and clients.

Need for a Major Paradigm Shift

What is required when we tackle a problem as big and as long standing as volunteer/staff relationships is a paradigm shift. I'm sure you've all encountered this concept. It's the catchword of the day in how to deal with a changing world. The longer I deal with creative problem solving, the more convinced I am that this concept is sound, workable and necessary when tackling big challenges.

In understanding the concept of paradigms, three images have been helpful to me:

1. The **lens** through which we see life—or any particular situation, problem or challenge.

2. Our **perceptual map**: A map of Atlanta may be a very good map, but it won't help me get around in Little Rock or Seattle. The map must be appropriate to our destination. As Scott Peck said in *The Road Less Traveled*, "our view of reality is like a map with which to negotiate the terrain of life. If the map is false and inaccurate, we generally will be lost. If the map is true and accurate, we will generally know where we are, and if we have decided where we want to go, we will generally know how to get there."[3]

3. Our **belief system** through which we filter and often distort data and information so it will fit what we already believe. "I wouldn't have seen it if I hadn't believed it" and other self-fulfilling prophecies.

As Stephen Covey says in *The Seven Habits of Highly Effective People*, "If we want to make significant quantum change, we need to work on our basic paradigms."[4] And, it seems to me, a problem that has been around for 20 years qualifies for this kind of major work.

One of the most useful models I've seen in bringing this idea into practical application was presented in an article by John Scherer entitled "The Change Process: A Matter of Belief," in *The Journal of Religion and Applied Behavior Sciences* (Winter, 1987):[5]

Your perceptual map: What you believe is "out there"

Field of focus: What you notice

Diagnosis: Your interpretation of "the facts"

Strategy: What you intend to accomplish

Action alternatives: Things you could do

Action

Let me give you an example of how this works in my personal life:
Last summer I took a few weeks off. The intent was to get off airplanes
and out of hotels for a while and enjoy my lovely mountain home
outside of Boulder, Colorado. I decided one thing I truly wanted to do
to enhance my time at home was plant my rock garden with all kinds
of lovely flowers. The difficulty every year we had tried this was that
the deer who "hung out" in our yard loved to eat the flowers even more
than I loved to look at them.

So, I went to the best mountain nursery, asked for the most deer-resistant
plants they had and also got their expert advice on how to keep deer
away from the blossoms. They advised me to:

1.   Add blood meal to the soil.

2.   Spray plants with Repel.

3.   Add cayenne pepper as insurance.

Reassured, I had the nursery help me plant an absolutely spectacular
flower garden. And for several days I sat on my deck, read, looked
down on my garden and was happy as a clam. But then I began to
notice there were fewer flowers. I was mystified, as I didn't see any deer
in the yard. Then one day as I was on my deck reading I heard a funny,
wheezing, coughing sound and I went to investigate. There stood a
deer chomping away at my flowers. You see, she had respiratory issues
and couldn't smell a thing!

I began to wage a battle to save my flowers, rushing out earlier and
earlier each morning, hating to leave the house for fear she'd invade
again and all the time missing the point that I was ruining my vacation.
So I changed my paradigm from "flowers are beautiful" to "deer are
beautiful," and I relaxed, read and watched my doe eat contentedly
through the summer. That's when I became convinced of the power of
paradigm shifts!

Next, I'd like to share an example of how I've used John Scherer's "Change
Process Model"[5] to help organizations work to improve volunteer/staff
relationships:

CURRENT MODEL	NEW MODEL
Your Perceptual Map (what's out there)	
Conflict in volunteer/staff relationships is inevitable.	Volunteers and staff can work as a synergistic team.
Volunteers perceive staff as the enemy.	Volunteers perceive staff as allies.
Field of Focus (what you notice)	
Someone is at fault	Staff and volunteers work together at problem solving issues.
Volunteers (the good guys) vs. staff (the bad guys)	
Diagnosis (interpreting the "facts")	
Volunteers believe staff attitudes are wrong.	Staff works to understand underlying reasons for resistance.
Volunteers believe staff is incompetent.	Explore reasons for this attitude. What is the role of the Volunteer Director?
STRATEGY (what you intend to accomplish)	
Staff will shape up.	Explore alternative ways to overcome the problems. Set mutual goals that encourage collaborative team efforts.
Action Alternative (things you can do)	
Convert to "our" way of thinking.	Train staff and volunteers in collaborative team building.
Ignore the problem.	

Understanding the problem

In line with the new paradigm, I suggest that to effectively problem solve, we must first try to understand the problem. Let's look briefly at some of the most frequently expressed reasons for staff resistance to volunteers:

- Previous bad experience with volunteers.
- Fear of loss of their jobs.
- Fear of decrease in the quality of service and loss of control.

- Lack of staff involvement in determining how volunteers will be involved, or why.
- Little or no involvement in writing job descriptions, interviewing or evaluating volunteers.
- Misconceptions about who volunteers are today and what skills they bring.
- Fear that volunteers are unreliable.
- Fear that today's skilled volunteer might do a job better than staff can do.
- Lack of training in how to delegate to volunteers and how to supervise them.
- Lack of reward system for staff if they utilize volunteers.

These are real concerns and we need to take them seriously. And the good news is, there is not one of them that can't be dealt with under our new paradigm.

Eight Steps to Collaborative Volunteer/Staff Team Building

Let's get practical about action alternatives you can take if you are serious about shifting your paradigm from "volunteer/staff problems are inevitable" to "volunteers and staff can work together as collaborative/synergistic teams." The particular action steps you would each take might vary, depending on what you are already doing well. I'd like to take these actions one at a time and elaborate a bit on each.

Step 1: Focus on mission.

If you were to ask each member of your volunteer/staff team the following simple questions, could they all give you the answers? If not, why not?

- Why do we exist as a team?
- What is our purpose or mission and is this written down?
- How do we help achieve the mission of the organization?

This is probably the single most common problem in volunteer and staff teams. We get task focused and obsessed with short-range crisis management and lose sight of the overall mission (or don't even know what it is). This is deadly.

Mission motivates – maintenance does not!

A fax that arrived at a corporate headquarters read: "No one in our facility has seen the corporate mission statement. Please send a copy." After a long delay, they received a reply: "Who wants it, and why?"

The mission of all of your organizations is to serve your clients. That is why both volunteers and staff are there. It's when we take our eyes off that goal that all the petty "turf stuff" begins to emerge.

So, if your team cannot answer the questions I just posed, start there and clearly define the mission of your team. And be sure each member knows the mission of your organization so that the team's purpose is compatible and supportive of it.

I have one bias: mission statements need to be short, snappy and inspiring. Avoid the long two- to three-page boring treatises, they don't motivate anyone.

Step 2: Determine clear objectives and action plans together.

Here is where collaboration starts or stops. Is the leader planning *with* or *for* the team? This is where ownership or "buy in" begins. A basic management principle is:

People become committed to plans they help make.

This step helps put good intentions (and lofty missions) into doable actions. It frees people up to know what to do and how to do it.

Remember the "SMAC" method of setting objectives. They should be:

Specific
Measurable
Achievable
Compatible

Writing clear objectives determines what you are going to do about your mission this year, specifically; the action plan determines the way it will be done. An action plan covers:

- Who is to do what.
- How they will do it.
- When it will be done (create a time line).
- Cost involved.

At this step, it is essential that you decide together not only what you will do (objectives/priorities), but also what you will *not do*. Everyone in this audience is confronted with an endless array of things you "could, should, might or ought to do." In times of scarce resources, it becomes vital to focus on a few essential priorities and do them well and that means letting go of things you've done in the past that were "nice, but not necessary." And that is hard. It is a matter of focusing resources on key priorities and your objectives are your priorities.

When these are mutually agreed upon by your volunteer and staff team, then you can begin to define clearly the roles, responsibilities and job descriptions. Everyone will then know their part to play and can get on with doing it without wasting endless hours trying to figure out "why am I here?" and "who's on first?" I-versus-they begins to become *us*!

Step 3: Participative/empowering leadership is essential.

Have you ever been on a team where the leaders (either volunteer or paid staff) thought leadership meant they decide and tell everyone else on the team what to do *and* how to do it? I'm sure that made you feel highly motivated, eager, creative and needed. Right? Wrong! This autocratic style of management was both prominent and successful in this country for a long time when we were an industrial nation of primarily blue collar workers and needed to run factories and huge bureaucracies. Most of the experts on the subject of effective leadership today agree that this style no longer works and, in fact, is becoming destructive and counter-productive. It encourages the parasitic, 1 + 1 = less than 2 type of teams. So, if our goal is collaborative/synergistic teams, the issue of leadership style becomes critical. Max DePree said,

> *The art of leadership is liberating people to do what is required of them in the most effective and humane way possible. It begins with a belief in the potential of people. Participative management without a belief in that potential and without convictions about the gifts people bring to organizations is a contradiction in terms.*[6]

Tom Peters, author of *In Search Of Excellence*, in an article about his experiences in working with leaders throughout the world stated that exceptional leaders have three traits in common:

- They know they can learn from anyone.
- They constantly look for 1,000 new small ways to improve what they already do well.
- They delight in the success of their subordinates.[7]

These are all descriptions of participative/empowering leaders and if you've ever had the pleasure of working with one of them you have no doubt experienced a truly synergistic team. Replicate it! If the leader is too busy doing most of the work, which is one of the traps in this field, there is neither time nor energy for this style of leadership.

Step 4: Determine, develop and utilize the strengths and skills of all team members.

Once again, let me share a quote from *Leadership Is An Art*, which deals with this important step: "It is fundamental that leaders endorse a concept of persons. This begins with an understanding of the diversity of people's gifts, talents and skills....Each of us is needed. We must admit we cannot know and do everything."[8]

Whenever I start a team or task force, I like to have a team building session as early in the process as possible. The purpose of this meeting is simply to help us know and understand more about one another so that we can maximize our strengths and minimize our weaknesses as a team. It's also how we begin to articulate our needs and hopes. A simple format I've used may be of help.

If the team is composed of a dozen or less people, I ask each one to take a few minutes and write down answers to four questions:

- What are two strengths (abilities/talents) I bring to this team?
- What are two weaknesses (things I don't do well) I bring to this team?
- My major concern for this team is…
- My major dream for this team is…

To debrief this exercise, it is vital that the leader shares her own answers first. (If you are honest, open and therefore vulnerable, your team will follow your lead; if you play games, so will they.) What you can end up with is a clear list of team strengths and weaknesses that will help you make sensible and creative decisions about work assignments and delegation. It becomes quickly apparent that synergy makes sense. We really can be better together than alone. The lists of concerns and dreams are the starting place for planning and problem-solving priorities.

One of the essential skills both volunteer and staff leaders must develop is the skill of effective delegation. We can have the greatest collection of skills and abilities on our team, but if we don't know how to share our work effectively we don't need teams at all. We just need to continue being heroic lone rangers until we burn out. (And when we leave, we take everything we know with us!)

We must deal honestly and seriously with the fact that today's volunteer work force is the most skilled, talented and varied we have ever had. We must personally, as volunteer administrators, learn to seek out and utilize these professional volunteers in our own departments and programs and see to it that other staff is trained to do so as well. Believe it or not, many paid staff are totally unaware of the revolution in our field as to who is volunteering, what they have to offer and why they're doing it.

So, we have new training challenges before us to help staff and volunteer leaders understand and accept today's volunteers as full partners on their teams and task forces. Some topics needing to be addressed are:

- trends in volunteerism
- delegation
- creative problem solving
- collaborative team building

Believe me when I say that your paid staff has not received training in any of these areas at their professional schools. Training is simply helping people succeed in what they have said "yes" to. So we must provide whatever training is needed for both volunteers and staff to be at their best.

Step 5: Develop creative problem-solving and decision-making skills.

I am often intrigued by how much we have forgotten as adults that we knew as kids. One of the biggest things is how to be creative. Let's compare the difference between how kids and adults usually solve a problem:

- The average group of adults gathers around a table and the leader grimly tells them a problem has arisen within their project. Faces get long and groans are heard as they say, "not another one." Up goes a flip chart and out come a few ideas. People then, too frequently, support the person proposing the idea instead of objectively exploring all the options and alternatives. Rarely does this system produce creative solutions. It falls into expediency.

- Now, let's gather a group of 5-year-olds and set up an obstacle course for them to conquer to get to the back of the room. The energy and sense of challenge and excitement is wonderful. They climb over, under, go around, laugh, maybe cry once in a while if they fall down but they have a wonderful time getting to the goal. I'm sure they didn't sit in a circle, put up a flip chart and ask, "Does anyone know how someone else has done this before?"

So the key to creative problem solving is really thinking in terms of **alternatives and options.** I conduct a week-long session on creative problem solving at the third level of the University of Colorado Volunteer Management Program each year. I have found a simple three-step process to be very helpful. (See "Influencing Outcomes You Care About" for full details.)

- **Clearly and creatively identify the problem to be solved and the goal to be achieved.**
  a. Be sure it's the real problem and not just a symptom.
  b. Have more than one alternative solution or option.
- **Strategize carefully.**
  c. Determine who can say yes or no to your proposed solution.
  d. Decide who, how and when to approach them and use the strengths of your team.
  e. Make your case effectively.
  f. Avoid getting no's because you didn't do your homework.
- **Negotiate effectively.**
  g. Listen to the needs and concerns of the other party.
  h. Be flexible and open to a new collaborative solution that helps you both win.

    i. Always concentrate on problem solving instead of blaming.

    j. View the other party as your ally not your enemy.

Step 6: Encourage and reward creativity and risk.

If we are to encourage and develop creativity in our teams—in planning, problem solving, decision making and carrying out their assignments, we must make it a valued group norm. That means, as a team we decide to not only tolerate, but encourage risk-taking and innovation.

DePree has a bit of wisdom here also: "We cannot become what we need to be by remaining what we are."[9] Someone else once said: "The enemy of the best is not the worst but the good enough." We all know groups and organizations that made the deadly mistake of resting on their past laurels and getting bogged down in the status quo. In today's changing world, they're going out of business at alarming rates. In times of decreasing resources, it will be happening to more and more of our programs that were effective "once upon a time."

And that is why what we are discussing today is so vital. It is usually the volunteer members of our teams that will have the most innovative and creative ideas because they see what we do with fresh eyes and new perspectives. They do not live with the problems eight to ten hours a day, five days a week as staff does. They have different skills and experiences to bring to bear on the problems and most of all, they are like persistent, inquisitive 5-year-olds, constantly asking those pesky "why" and "why not" questions that we hate, but desperately need to hear.

So the key to this step is encourage and support your team's new ideas, try out the most promising ones, celebrate together when ideas succeed and learn from them if they fail.

Step 7: Evaluate the work of the team objectively and honestly.

Evaluation is simply examining periodically your "well done's" and your opportunities to improve.

Objective evaluation becomes easy when you have steps 1 and 2 in place—a clear mission statement and specific, measurable objectives with action plans that clarify who is responsible for what, how, when and costs. You simply measure your performance against these stated goals and decide:

1. Did we do what we said we would, on time and within budget? If not, why not? And what do we intend to do to correct the situation (problem solving)?

2. Then you take a look at each member's job descriptions and assignments and give them timely and honest feedback regarding their "well done's" and "opportunities to improve"?

3. Did you each keep your commitments to one another as a team? (It is vital to hold one another accountable and not rescue or ignore unacceptable behavior or continual failure to perform agreed upon assignments—it is deadly for the morale of the group.)

4. How do you celebrate your successes together? The really healthy people of the world know when to "yes," when to say "no" and when to say "whoopee!" How do you say whoopee as a team?

It is essential that when the work is done as a volunteer/staff team that *all* members of the team are recognized by the organization equally. One of the major complaints I hear from paid staff is that their agencies so often recognize volunteer contributions with pins, plaques and parties but staff's only reward is getting a paycheck and staying in the background. Evaluation forms for paid staff should include "ability to work effectively with volunteers" and their raises and promotions should be influenced by that factor. When this becomes common practice, we will see staff attitudes toward volunteers change dramatically. Also, as letters of appreciation are encouraged to go from staff to volunteers, the reverse is also important.

Step 8: Create and maintain a healthy climate.

Good collaborative teams value, respect, and appreciate one another. And they have fun together. This is what creates and maintains a healthy organizational climate. Climate is simply how it feels to be there, and it's apparent how important this is when we have volunteers on the team. Why should a person volunteer to work in a place or with a group that makes them feel bad…and do it for nothing? The fact is, unless they are masochistic, they leave.

A few of the key components that determine the climate of any organization or group within it are the following:

Structure: That is how many rules, regulations, layers of hierarchy and how much red tape is there. The less the better!

Leadership style: This is the most important factor in determining the climate. Give people the feeling of being their own bosses. Treat them as responsible and valuable members of the team.

Warmth and support: The team collaborates on work to be done rather than getting hung up on roles and turf. Pitching in and helping one another becomes the norm.

Standards: Caring enough about what we are doing to be at our best.

Conflict management: Disagreements and differences are brought to the surface and dealt with rather than denying or smoothing them over or letting them go underground. Conflicts that are not dealt with will *always* resurface.

Strong sense of identity and belonging: All members know why the team is together, their roles and responsibilities and feel a sense of pride and purpose in being part of the team.

To summarize what collaborative teams of volunteers and staff can and should be, I'd like to share a quote from *How Can I Help?* by Ram Dass and Paul Gorman: "The reward, the real grace, of conscious service is the opportunity not only to help relieve suffering but to grow in wisdom, experience greater unity and have a good time while we're doing it."[10]

[1] William Dyer, *Team Building* (Addison-Wesley, 1987), 20.

[2] Max DePree, *Leadership Is an Art* (Dell, 1989), xx.

[3] M. Scott Peck, *The Road Less Traveled* (Simon and Schuster, 1978), 44.

[4] Stephen Covey, *The Seven Habits of Highly Effective People* (Free Press, 1989), 44.

[5] John Scherer, "The Change Process: A Matter of Belief," in *The Journal of Religion and Applied Behavior Sciences*, (Winter, 1987).

[6] DePree, *op. cit.*, xx.

[7] Tom Peters and Robert Waterman Jr., *In Search of Excellence* (Harper Collins, 1982).

[8] DePree, *op. cit.*, 9.

[9] Ibid., 44.

[10] Ram Dass and Paul Gordon, *How Can I Help?* (Alfred A. Knopf, 1985), 16.

How to Perk Up Your Presentations
Using Stories, Metaphors, and Quotes

International Conference on Volunteer Administration
Dallas, TX, October, 1998

Have you ever stopped and tried to analyze something you've done for a very long time and it has become almost second nature to you? That's kind of how I feel about this topic. I have given hundreds of speeches and workshops over the past three decades (and many of you have been in a lot of them). Some have been terrific (she says modestly!), some mediocre and, honestly, there are a few I'd like to pretend never happened.

The question that now intrigues me is—what made the difference? Another question is, what do people remember out of all those words and therefore, what has had a lasting impact?

The common denominator that emerges as I contemplate the best presentations is that the information and concepts were liberally illustrated with metaphors, stories, and quotes. When I let my natural love of storytelling keep my logical, rational left brain under control, the speech or workshop changes from being a contest to see how much information I could cram in (and in turn impress my audience with) to a chance to communicate ideas and concepts I'm excited about with people I truly care about.

The principle that makes all the difference is this: **You have not communicated if your audience has not received your message!** And, the best way to accomplish this is to shift the focus from me (the presenter), to you (the audience).

Another thing I began to notice is that the quality of the communication for me (and the audience) improved dramatically when we were having fun in the process of the learning. Erma Bombeck once said, "Laughing is like internal jogging." Laughing creates endorphins, which increases energy, which increases the ability to learn and remember. For me, there is nothing more fun than creating word pictures and images that can take a complex concept and "bring it on home" to the audience. I love seeing eyes light up and smiles emerge and the "a-ha" phenomenon happen. That's the elixir for any speaker and it's what keeps us doing it! The truth is, it's the images (metaphors and stories) that people tell me they remember years later.

How about those other presentations—the mediocre and the boring ones. Why do they happen when I know better? What I've learned is there is a direct correlation between the quality of my presentations and my own emotional and physical well-being. Charles Garfield (author of *Peak Performance*) said, "You don't go through life 'motivating' people; you 'jumpstart' them. And you can't jumpstart anyone unless your own battery is charged!"[1]

My presentations suffered before and during the three times I've come very close to burn out.

1. While trying to finish *Survival Skills for Managers* in the early 1980s.
2. Before my nine-month sabbatical in 1994.
3. The months before my stroke in May of 1998.

A-ha! Now I see my pattern:

Doing creative/innovative work (writing/speeches/workshops)
... *which leads to*

Increased demand/invitations/challenges and too many "yes's" (overworked) ... *which leads to*

Pressure (from me and others) to continue to be creative and eventually becoming blocked by overwork in doing so ... *which leads to*

Escalating the energy to keep going and do "good work" in spite of fatigue ... *which leads to*

Frantic pace that ends up in mechanical/non-creative work
... *which starts to*

"Kill me" (the soul goes out of my work) ... *and finally*

Caught in this destructive cycle, I lose the ability/energy/openness to see or use the metaphors and stories (even though they're still all around me).

That's when it all becomes left-brained, informational and mechanical. It loses heart and soul and thus becomes work and the joy and fun goes out of it all. And, voila—mediocre, less effective workshops and burn out for me. Julia Cameron, author of *The Artists Way*, says, "The truth is that work can dry up because it is going well."[2]

Metaphors

Let's try using a metaphor to help us understand all the options we have as speakers/presenters re: delivering the "goods" (our message).

My Speech 101 teacher in college was adamant about one particular thing—he said he wanted to be able to see right straight through from the beginning to the end of any speech. In other words, he wanted us to get from point A to point B, clearly, cleanly, with no side trips.

Moving from point A to point B makes me think of travel so I'm going to use the metaphor of highways to illustrate different ways to get from point A to point B in our speeches.

Route #1: The Super Highway

Imagine all the types of vehicle drivers (speakers) you've listened to on this type of journey. Here are some examples:

- **Semi truck driver**—big, powerful, fast, important—time is money.
- **Sports car driver**—using all the bells and whistles—using all gimmicks, fads and clichés—a show.
- **Cell phone users**—the person on the other end of the phone is more important than the audience—distracted, not quite there.
- **Boom box player**—it's all just noise.
- **Lost-the-way driver**—looking at the map while driving (notes mixed up, lost) "I don't know where we are Mabel, but we're sure making good time."
- **Good solid economy car driver**—no nonsense—get there safely and on time (but boring!).

Route #2: Country Roads

We might get off the super highway in pure frustration and end up meandering along some country roads. The problem is we don't know where we are and neither does the audience. It may be entertaining and enjoyable, but not a learning experience.

Let me share a true story with you:

One of the most creative, right-brained presenters I've ever met was a pastor named Warren Salveson. Warren, Marianne Wilkerson, and I created a two-day training program for Lutheran churches called "Mobilizing Church Volunteers." We traveled the U.S. together delivering our program and it was highly successful. Warren always led off our sessions. His speeches were always full of wonderful stories and metaphors and our audiences loved him. The problem was every time he spoke, Marianne and I never knew where he was headed with his speech as it always went in a different direction. Our challenge was to follow him and try to make our sessions tie into where his speech had taken the audience.

Years later, I shared with Warren about how much I learned from him about the power of stories and metaphors. I also lovingly told him what trouble we had doing the follow-up sessions because we weren't sure where he was going. He laughed and said, "You know, I learned a lot from you two, also. I learned it was good to have an outline, and it's helped my effectiveness in preaching. For years people have told me they enjoy my sermons—but now they also tell me they understand them!"

Route #3: Travel the Blue Highways

Are you the type of person who plans out your trip and highlights the route on the map before you leave? This is what I mean by "blue highways." To get from point A to point B using a clearly marked map (outline) you not only know your destination but can enjoy the journey.

To do this, we use all our senses and engage the audience, too. When I prepare a presentation, I keep the following points in mind so I'm sure to engage all of people's senses:

- **Sight**—use DVDs, videos, PowerPoint™ presentations and handouts (attractive and colorful)
- **Imagination**—metaphors, stories and quotes
- **Sounds**—laughter, one another (participants)
- **Relief stops**—that's what some stories, humor, quotes are for…to change the pace…let people catch their breath…connect.

But, as you choose what to use, remember the admonition of my good friend and master trainer, Arlene Schindler. Arlene says, in training, there's neither right nor wrong, there's only appropriate or inappropriate. And, in order to determine what is appropriate, it's essential to "read" your audience constantly.

Reading your audience is like reading the river in river rafting. My son, Richard, worked one summer in college as a river raft guide in Colorado. He wanted our family to come on one of his trips so my husband, Harvey, and daughter, Lisa, and I went (I more reluctantly than the other two). We were peacefully floating along the Colorado River when all of a sudden the sound of the river became a roar and some large, ferocious looking rapids appeared ahead of us. Rich oared our raft over to the bank, got out and climbed to where he had a good view of the rapids. He watched quietly for several minutes and finally I asked him, "What are you doing?" He replied, "I'm reading the river, Mom. Some of our guides haven't learned how to spot the currents and eddies and they've gotten into real trouble when they try to shoot the rapids."

Marlene and her husband, Harvey

If we don't read the river (our audience) we can make inappropriate choices, not just about the stories, but about format and process, and get into real trouble, too.

Quotes

As many of you know, I use quotations a lot, in both my writing and speaking. People often ask me why and especially, why don't I change a word here and there and call it my own. When someone has already said it "just right" my feeling is why tinker with it? And, it's "just right" in my opinion when I'm reading along and I find that sentence or phrase that stops me in my tracks, or I catch my breath and utter an admiring "I wish I'd said that!" Mark Twain said, "The difference between the right word and the almost right word is the difference between lightning and a lightning bug."

The creativity comes in determining just where and how to share the quote so others can enjoy and be impacted by it. I always give credit to the author so people can go to the source and read more. It helps that I love to read and usually keep cards or a notebook for quotes as I go. Currently I have about five huge file folders and I look forward to revisiting them to search for forgotten gems!

I'd like to share some favorite phrases, one-liners and quotes. When I know the source, I've given credit.

"Just right" phrases:
- "Life is like an onion, you peel it off one layer at a time and sometimes you weep." —Carl Sandburg
- "Live simply that others may simply live." —Gandhi

- "The really mentally and emotionally healthy people are those who have learned when to say 'yes' when to say 'no' and when to say 'whoopee'!" —Willard Krabell, M.D.
- "When it's dark enough you can see the stars." —Charles Barnes
- "You cannot be creative if you don't dare risk, you cannot risk if you don't dare fail, it is not failure if you learn from it."
  —Harvey Wilson
- "Leaders are painters of the vision and architects of the journey."
  —Joe Nevin

One-liners:

- "Nobody likes change but a wet baby."
- "Some people suffer in silence louder than other people."
- "You can't just go on being a good egg; you've either got to hatch or go bad." —C.S. Lewis in *Mere Christianity*
- "Retire at 65...that's ridiculous! I was still getting pimples!"
  —George Burns
- "The only difference between a rut and a grave is how deep it is.
  —Hugh Chalmers, President Chalmers Motor Car Company

Favorite quotes:

- "If the only prayer we ever prayed our whole life was 'thank you,' that would be enough." —Meister Eckhart
- "To feel that what we do is right for ourselves and good for the world at the exactly same time is one of the great triumphs of human existence." —David Whyte, *Crossing the Unknown Sea*
- "Leaving the work to find its own place in the world is the mark of a good workman and good workwoman." —David Whyte
- "Our work is to make ourselves visible in the world. This is the soul's individual journey and the soul would much rather fail at its own life than succeed at someone else's." —David Whyte
- "In the soil of the quick fix is the seed of a new problem, because our quiet wisdom is unavailable." —Wayne Muller, *Sabbath*
- "All life has emptiness at its core, it is the quiet hollow reed through which the wind of God blows and makes the music that is our life. Without that emptiness we are clogged and unable to give birth to music, love and kindness." —Wayne Muller
- "In pursuit of knowledge, every day something is acquired. In pursuit of wisdom, every day something is dropped." —Lao Tzu
- "We are most deeply asleep at the switch when we fancy we control any switch at all." —Annie Dillard

- "We are the ending of some stories, the carrying on of others and often, just the beginning of many it is not our place to finish."
—David Whyte

Stories

As openers:

Starting a speech with a story is a tried and true strategy. Why stories? They:

- Set the audience at ease
- Establish rapport
- Help the audience see this may be fun—as well as informative
- Eliminate distance between us

Here's a story I use frequently. It a story about Will Rogers, one of America's most beloved humorists who spoke and served as master of ceremonies at hundreds of events.

At a banquet Will was asked to introduce the after dinner speaker, which he did. The speaker was very enamored with his topic (as I tend to be about volunteerism). The people were still sitting at their tables and Rogers could see them beginning to fall asleep as the speaker went on and on. After a few heads actually landed on the tables, Rogers decided he had to do something as the emcee. So, he cleared his throat loudly to get the speaker's attention. The speaker then apologized for speaking so long. He said, "Oh, I'm sorry, I forgot my watch." Will Rogers responded, "It's a shame you didn't notice the calendar right behind you!"

I use this story when beginning an after-dinner speech, and then take off my watch and hold it up assuring the audience I have one.

To change pace and illustrate a concept:

You'll see that I use stories and quotes liberally to change pace or illustrate a concept. My audiences particularly respond to true stories that happened to me. For example in "Influencing Outcomes You Care About," I use a story about my son Rich and his imaginary childhood friend, George, to illustrate a concept about the use of imagination. The presentation on "Motivation" is full of true examples that illustrate how readers can apply the principles to involve volunteers effectively.

These are good ways to "jump start" the audience if energy begins to wane. As you begin to hone your skills at reading your audience, the challenge is to stay flexible and be versatile. Like a skilled dancer, you need to move with ease between options and still be true to your goal of getting from point A to point B! Don't keep doing what isn't working.

The Power of Metaphors

Did anyone struggle with the concept of metaphors in high school English? Basically, metaphors are an attempt to say something about the unfamiliar in terms that are familiar. I like to think of metaphors as word pictures; they help the listener visualize a concept.

Sources of metaphors

Once you start thinking about metaphors, you'll find them all around you and make connections to other things you are doing.

Here's a story that shows how I translated a real-life experience into a metaphor that I use to illustrate the concept of creating achievable objectives.

My daughter, Lisa, and I were on a mountain vacation and wanted to go on a hike. We had a guide and as we began to climb he pointed out our destination, a deserted mine about three-quarters of the way up a very steep mountain. I immediately wanted to give up the venture and turn back. I really didn't think I was in good enough shape to make it. The guide assured me that I could because there were many switchbacks (short zigzagging trails) all the way up the climb. Two hours later, I stood triumphantly at the mine looking down into the valley shouting, "I did it!"

In training, I use this story to show that if we provide good, achievable short-range plans or objectives (switchbacks) we are much more apt to eventually arrive at our long-range goals without burning out or feeling defeated.

Conclusion

I hope it's now apparent that appropriate stories, metaphors and quotes not only make presentations more colorful and fun (for you and your audience) but, even more importantly, they help make complex concepts come alive so they become both useful and memorable! Which reminds me of a story!

Two nuns were riding down a country road late one night when they ran out of gas. One of them walked to a farmhouse they'd passed and asked the farmer if he had some gas they could use. He said he had some but didn't have a gas can. The nun and the farmer went into the barn to see what they could find to carry the gas. They found an old, rusty bedpan, filled it with gas and carried it back to the car. Just as they were starting to pour the gas in the tank, a car came by. The driver slowed, rolled down his window and exclaimed, "Ma'am, I don't know what religion you are, but you sure do have faith!"

Have faith in yourself and your audience.

---

[1]Charles Garfield, *Peak Performance* (Grand Central Publishing, 1989), 27.

[2] Julia Cameron, *The Artists Way* (J.P. Tarcher/Putnam, 2002), 21.

What Are You Marketing?
VISION Is the Job of Leadership

University of Colorado Volunteer Management Certificate Program
Boulder, CO, July 1986

Most hierarchies are nowadays so encumbered with rules and traditions, and so bound in by public laws, that even high employees do not have to lead anyone anywhere, in the sense of pointing out the direction and setting the pace. They simply follow precedents, obey regulations, and move at the head of the crowd. Such employees lead only in the sense that the carved wooden figurehead leads the ship.

—The Peter Principle [1]

Perhaps this quote helps us understand the deeply disturbing conclusions that Bennis and Nanus point out in their recent book, *Leaders: The Strategies for Taking Charge:*

- Fewer than one in four job holders in America is working at full potential.
- 75% of workers say they can be much more effective than they are.
- More and more employees are doing their most creative things away from the workplace (such as avocations and hobbies).[2]

What we are seeing is a wide-spread followers revolt and in profit, non-profit and public organizations alike. Why? Bennis summarizes it well: "Leaders have failed to instill vision, meaning and trust in their followers."[3]

In other words, leaders have forgotten to lead. In *A Passion for Excellence,* Peters and Austin say:

The basics got lost in a blur of well meaning gibberish that took us further and further from excellent performance in any sphere. We got so tied up in our techniques, devices and programs that we forgot about people—the people who produce the product or service and the people who consume it…what are the basics of managerial success? Two of the most important are pride in one's organization and enthusiasm for its works.[4]

In other words, we somehow got so enamored with the process that we forgot our people—we got so wrapped up in day-to-day crises that we lost sight of the mission!

The result has been too many uninspired, disillusioned workers, like the one who recently gave up coffee said, "Nowadays I really don't want to be that wide awake." The hopeful news is that there seems to be a revolution also occurring in the whole arena of leadership and leadership training. The new literature flooding our bookstores—and hopefully the MBA classrooms and schools of sociology, psychology and theology—are filled with a whole new set of terms:

- Core Values
- Vision
- Mission
- Love
- Trust
- Nurturing
- Coaching

In *A Passion for Excellence* we read: "We advocate a change from 'tough-mindedness' to 'tenderness', from hard data and balance sheets to a concern for the 'soft stuff', values, vision and integrity."[5]

Let's examine for a moment a few definitions, so we can get a little "meat on the bones" of these important terms, and concepts.

Core Values:

The essence of an organization's philosophy about what is success and how it should be achieved and measured. (A new kind of bottom line.) Core values often can be stated in slogans which have become the rallying cry of all who work there:

Sears Roebuck: "Quality at a good price."

Dana Corp.: "Productivity through people."

SAS: "Fifty million moments of truth each year" turned the corporation totally around in three years.

Surgeon General: "A smokeless society by the year 2000."

Vision

"A vision is a target that beckons."

"A vision is a mental journey from the known to the unknown."

In *Creating Excellence,* the authors' state, "Today's success story requires a new type of leader. We call those leaders 'new age executives'...They develop a vision for their organization and they master the skills to implement that vision."[6] (Please note the core values and vision come first, before implementation of plans.) As someone put it, "that keeps the gunk from getting in the way of important stuff." In my opinion, that's exactly where we have gone astray. We started to dance before we knew what the music was and we too often got miserably out of step!

Mission

John Naisbitt asks, "What business are you in?"[7] I believe no organization will survive that can't answer that question! A clear statement of purpose (based on values and vision) is the beginning of turning dreams into reality. This mission needs to be clearly articulated by the leadership and shared with everyone who works there!

Goal: A Dream with Deadlines

It's here that the necessary skills of implementation should bring dreams to fruition. It's why learning to plan, organize, staff, direct and control are so important...not because that's what you have to do to be a manager, but that's what you do to help people make dreams happen.

May I suggest an analogy? The core values and vision are the *heart* of an organization. The missions, goals, and plans are the *guts* of an organization. We get sick organizations when they end up either heartless or gutless!

Defining Your Mission

I suggest one approach may be to go backwards before you try to go forwards. What I mean by this is all of our organizations were founded by people who had a compelling vision and mission and had to care passionately about it in order to be able to achieve that mission. It took energy, patience, marketing and persistence to birth an organization or agency.

Do you know what the original mission and vision was? If not, try to find out. It's a good place to start. Wipe out disease, feed the hungry, support the dying and their families, teach the handicapped to be independent, provide equal opportunity in the work place—what was the cause as your founders articulated it?

Here's one of my own examples. When I became involved in what was to become the Volunteer and Information Center of Boulder County in the 1960s, our vision was to match up the needs in our community with the resources were knew were out there. We marketed ourselves this way and dared to ask anyone for anything to help us get the job done. As the founders, we had that zeal and it permeated and inspired our whole group. It was a fantastic experience.

Does your cause need to be rearticulated or re-defined to be appropriate now? If so, how and why?

Hospitals that think of themselves as being only there to take care of sick people (in the "sick business") will be out of business. Those who have re-defined their mission as being in the "health business" have a good chance of surviving and thriving.

How can you involve present leaders in this process of redefining mission? At corporate giant Johnson & Johnson, the leadership had little knowledge or acceptance of the corporate mission statement that was written a decade earlier. They took all members of top management on a retreat and their only agenda was to redefine the mission statement. They took the original one and for two days tore it apart, argued, debated and finally defined their own mission statement. The astounding thing was, it turned out to be identical to the original one. The difference was, now they owned it. It does not work until it's owned!

I believe in the 1960s and 1970s many human service agencies began to become lazy about their missions. It had to do with the easy availability of grants. It was too tempting to add programs, not because they were ways to achieve the central mission and purpose, or that they were desperately needed, but because that's where the money was. Many organizations I worked with began to look like amoebas—with little program pieces tacked on here and there until even the staff couldn't tell you the mission, let alone the vision or core values. Now that those grants are gone, the groups that are staying healthy are those that stayed clear about their basic mission and did that well. They know what cause they are marketing and it is more than survival or "help us or we'll go down the tubes." In marketing terms it's called "knowing your marketing niche" instead of trying to be all things to all people.

How about vision? How do we help ourselves and others to become more visionary? May I suggest two wonderful books that might help you get out of ruts, both personal and organizational? *A Whack on the Side of the Head* and *A Kick in the Seat of the Pants*, both by Roger von Oech. In *A Kick in the Seat of the Pants,* von Oech outlines the four critical roles of the creative thinker (and you can't be a visionary without being creative). I'd like to explore these roles with you.

Explorer

When you are an explorer you are searching for the materials, information and experiences to make new ideas. Information is abundant. Do your homework.

Artist

As an artist you take the explorer's materials and transform them into original new ideas. This is the imaginative and playful part.

Judge

The judge evaluates and examines objectively and honestly what your artist created and decides whether to implement, modify or discard it. Don't discard something just because you are scared.

Warrior

The warrior is the doer who carries the idea from the world of "what if" to the world of "what is." You become part general and part foot soldier. You develop the strategy and plans and have the discipline to slug it out in the trenches and the passion to keep going when things get tough. Here's where the marketing comes in. If you don't sell your ideas they die. How many good ideas have not come to fruition because the person could not sell them? Winston Churchill once said, that the most important lesson life had taught him was never give up, never give up, never give up. Another person put it this way, "Either you let your life slip away by not doing the things you want to do, or you get up and do them!"[8]

What is the dream with your name on it? When you know, become the explorer, artist, judge and warrior for that one dream and you will make a difference.

When speaking of vision there's always the difficulty of juggling the perspective of the big picture with the realities of things closer at hand, the needs of today and tomorrow. Two experiences I've had in the past few months illustrate this:

On a vacation to Greece my husband, Harvey and I went parasailing. It was a whole new and fresh view of things and definitely a stretch for me personally. The experience gave me a whole new perspective on the world. Flying over the beach I was totally removed from mundane worries and daily humdrum. My mind soared along with my body. When I thought about it later I realized that what parasailing taught me was how to see the big picture.

On the same trip we went snorkeling and it was the opposite experience of parasailing. In snorkeling I had to stick my head under water (under the surface.) The entire amazing world lying right under the surface of the water and still it was so easy to look at the big ocean and miss it! How much of our time do we miss the incredible creativity and resourcefulness of the people right in front of our noses because we're not looking for it!

We need to be people of vision and, I might add, both experiences were a bit scary. I had to be willing to risk trying something new or I'd have missed out. Creativity and risk go together!

I would suggest that some of the most critical challenges before human service agencies and everyone it the nonprofit world in the next couple of years is to carefully re-think how we choose our leaders and what we define as our core values.

What are the criteria we use for selecting nominating committees and boards of directors? What are the qualities we look for in our executives and managers? (Vision is the job of leadership!) What do we reward throughout the organization—status quo or innovation?

It is in dealing with these serious questions that the core values of an organization become apparent.

How Do You Market an Organization's Vision and Mission to Your Staff, Volunteers and Clients?

First of all, identify and define it and secondly share it with every single person who serves with or is served by you. This one you don't want to hide under a bushel basket. It is the mission that motivates! Let's look at an example of a motivating mission and its affect on those involved: the Apollo 11 Project.

When the Grumman Aerospace Corp. was given the mission to design and build the first manned space craft to land on the moon, thousands of very ordinary, reasonably successful men and women woke up and performed miracles. The challenge of pushing back the frontiers of space and putting Americans on the moon was articulated to all employees in every conceivable way (posters, slogans, symbols, speeches, articles). One long-time employee said:

I've been a piece of furniture in my job for years. Do you know what it's like working 40-60 hours a week and not knowing whether your work makes a damn bit of difference to anybody? People have been dreaming about going to the moon for thousands of years. And we're going to do it! You want to know why we're doing so well. Want to know my secret? I've got a mission, something that matters to me, something that matters to all of us. We finally got something we can sink our teeth into and be proud of! [9]

Peak performances begin with a commitment to a mission!

What an incredibly important lesson for us to learn and re-learn. How do we motivate people? We define missions that matter. There is no group in the world that has more important, more compelling missions than we do in this room—to alleviate suffering, to improve the quality of life, to feed the hungry and comfort the dying. Let's get back to clarifying, articulating and passionately sharing those missions with our people.

A poignant example of the reverse of this is illustrated by a story told by Zig Zigler. It's a story about a trainer of fleas. The trainer described the very simple process he used. Get a jar, put some fleas in it and then put the lid on the jar (after punching in some air holes). Then just sit and watch.

The fleas will spend several days trying to jump out of the jar and they'll keep bumping their heads on the lid. Finally they learn to stop about an inch below the lid and that way they won't get hurt. After awhile you can even take the lid off and they will not jump out—they keep jumping only an inch from the top. After all, that's what they've been trained to think they can do! (How often have we limited people by our own limited expectations?) *If you think you can or if you think you can't—you're right!*

How do you market your cause to others?

There really are no shortcuts or strategies or marketing techniques that will replace the three absolute essentials:

1. A mission that matters
2. Turned-on staff and volunteers
3. Well-served clients

I agree with the statement in *A Passion for Excellence:* "It's all about attention. Attention is all there is!"[10] So the question for us to ponder as we leave this place is, what are we paying attention to? Vision and mission or survival? Motivating people or controlling them? Providing service or finding excuses? Leading or managing?

I can well imagine one of the greatest frustrations many of you are feeling right now is that you are not the key executive on the board of directors or president of your organization. You're probably a mid-management staff person or a volunteer who may be the chairperson of a committee. How can you make this kind of difference in your own organization?

I'd like to suggest we think for a moment about "'pockets." We've all heard phrases lately like "pockets of poverty," "pockets of despair," or "pockets of unemployment." What would happen if we all went home and became:

- Pockets of hope
- Pockets of innovation
- Pockets of commitment to missions that matter
- Pockets of renewed faith in the creativity and ability of ourselves and our people

My guess is that we'd soon find those pockets getting fuller and fuller. Do we have the faith to try it?

I have always believed that no matter what field I worked in that there is much to learn from other fields. The profession of volunteer management is so eclectic (for me that's part of its strength and fascination) that I have found reading books like the following help stretch my thinking and add to my competency. Check out some of these books (and you may want to give them as gifts to some executives you know).

Creating Excellence by Hickman and Silva

Peak Performers by Charles Garfield

Corporate Cultures by Deal and Kennedy

In Search of Excellence by Peters and Waterman

A Passion for Excellence by Peters and Austin

The Change Masters by Rosabeth Moss Kanter

Servant Leadership by Robert Greenleaf

Let me close with the poem "Autobiography in Five Short Chapters" by Portia Nelson:

I

I walk down the street.
There is a deep hole in the sidewalk.
I fall in.
I am lost...I am helpless.
It isn't my fault.
It takes me forever to find a way out.

II

I walk down the same street.
There is a deep hole in the sidewalk.
I pretend I don't see it.
I fall in again.
I can't believe I am in the same place

but, it isn't my fault.
It still takes a long time to get out.

III

I walk down the same street.
There is a deep hole in the sidewalk.
I see it is there.
I still fall in...it's a habit.
My eyes are open.
I know where I am.
It is my fault.
I get out immediately.

IV

I walk down the same street.
There is a deep hole in the sidewalk.
I walk around it.

V

I walk down another street.

[1] Laurence J. Peter and Raymond Hull, *The Peter Principle* (Pan Books, 1970).

[2] Warren Bennis and Burt Nanus, *Leaders: Strategies for Taking Charge* (Harper & Row, 1985).

[3] Ibid.

[4] Thomas J. Peters and Nancy Austin, *A Passion for Excellence* (Random House, 1985), xviii.

[5] Ibid., xix.

[6] Craig Hickman and Michael Silva, *Creating Excellence* (Plume, 1986).

[7] John Naisbitt, *Megatrends: ten directions of transforming our lives* (Warner Books, 1982).

[8] Roger von Oech, *A Kick in the Seat of the Pants* (Harper & Row, 1985), 11.

[9] Charles Garfield, *Peak Performance* (William Morrow & Co., 1986), 24-26.

[10] Peters and Austin, op. cit., 99.

Leading with Soul and Vision

University of Colorado Volunteer Management Certificate Program
Boulder, CO, July 1996

You will be spending the next few days exploring, learning and practicing essential skills and techniques to help you manage a successful volunteer program. We will cover the *what* and *how* questions to help you succeed. I want to begin this morning with a different question: Why do you want to manage a volunteer program in the first place?

Since this is the first of three levels in this certificate program, it is probably safe to assume most of you are either new to the profession of volunteer administration; have experience in another organization but are starting a new volunteer program at a new place; or you have inherited a failing program and have been hired to shape it up.

In any of those instances, I can promise you that you are facing an exciting, sometimes daunting challenge fraught with ups and downs, successes and setbacks, endless need and diminishing resources. So, it is vital that you begin with a clear answer in your own mind and heart about why you do it in the first place. It is what you can use as your beacon to keep you moving forward and your anchor in the midst of difficulties.

When this University of Colorado Volunteer Management Certificate Program began 25 years ago, there was only one book in the field (Harriet Naylor's *Volunteers Today*) and no training programs available for the small cadre of people designated as volunteer directors. That is the reason we began the Volunteer Management Certificate Program. As the field grew and resources multiplied, we added two more levels to try to meet the more complex needs of a maturing profession. I have been privileged to be a part of the development of this field for almost 30 years and, as I look back, I rejoice in the healthy proliferation of tools, techniques, books and workshops now available to help all of you do your jobs well. I also worry a bit about how we may have focused so intently on the *whats* and *hows* that the *why* questions have been neglected—or lost in the crush of crisis management.

So, we shall spend this time together talking about that very thing and thus my inclusion of the words *vision* and *soul* in my title. Those concepts deal with the *whys* of what we do. And more importantly, of *who* we are.

One of my favorite stories is about Justice Oliver Wendell Holmes. Supposedly, when he was in his 80s, he was riding on the Pennsylvania Railroad and he lost his ticket. As the conductor approached him, Holmes started madly searching through his pockets for his ticket. Finally, he admitted to the conductor that he couldn't find the ticket. The conductor recognized Justice Holmes, smiled and said it was all right and to mail the ticket to the railroad when he found it. Holmes looked at the conductor and said, "That's not the problem, my man...I need to know where I am going."

In 1994, I took a sabbatical year and re-examined my own vision for the field of volunteerism. (You can read about that year in detail in "Musings of a Chronologically Gifted Crone.") After months of pondering, journaling, and exploring options, my personal answer to "where am I going and why?" came back as a simple, but clear articulation of vision. Most helpful in doing this was re-visiting why I had gone into volunteer management in the first place. When I did so, my energy and commitment were rekindled and my soul was renewed. Yes! My answer is I do still believe in the unique purpose of what we do.

But perhaps it's time to look for new ways to serve the field I love. These words in David Whyte's *The Heart Aroused* struck me:

> We take the road of mid-life not as the beginning of disengagement and retirement, but as a newer, more powerful path to meaningful work, the work of belonging in a deeper way to those people and things we have learned to love. The task of mid-life is that task of finding the difficult often dangerous road to this eldership of love.[1]

To me, this is an excellent vision for our maturing profession and for those of us who have been in this field for a long time. Learning again, exploring again—searching again for still new avenues of service that can use our years of experience and whatever wisdom we have acquired along the way.

So what did I discover that I personally believe is the vision and purpose of volunteerism and volunteer management: I believe we are about *the business of creating in a world filled with destruction*:

- We create opportunities for people to be at their best through helping others.

- We create new meaning and purpose in people's lives by helping them discover and use their God-given talents and abilities and make a difference!
- We create hope for those experiencing life's difficulties. They learn that others do care.
- We create moments and pockets of real community and collaboration in a lonely, often hostile world. We demonstrate that titles, roles, gender, color and age do not matter when we are working together for causes we care about deeply.

I urge each of you to define your own vision or personal statement of purpose and revisit it often. Post it on your desk or computer. To begin the process, ask yourself, "Why did I say 'yes' to the job of volunteer manager? Has this reason changed?" Once your vision is clear and compelling, then you must continue to hone your management skills to enable that dream to be realized. That is what this certificate program is all about!

It is essential that we be concerned about vision in an era when human and social needs continue to escalate and resources diminish at alarming rates. Many experts predict that there will be a dramatic paradigm shift in how we meet social needs. That is, that nonprofits and churches—instead of the government—will be the primary providers of care. It is already happening, as you all know.

Peter Drucker, one of the world's leading management scholars, in a powerful article in the The Wall Street Journal entitled "It Profits Us to Strengthen the Non-profits" made the following observations:

- Nonprofits have the potential to become America's social sector, equal in importance to the public sector (government) and the private sector (business).
- Nonprofits spend less for results than the government spends for failures in meeting human needs.
- It is essential that the average nonprofit manage itself well and give up the belief that good intentions and a pure heart are all that are needed. They must be accountable for performance and results.[2]

Drucker points out that there are now over 900,000 nonprofits. They have become America's largest employer, and the vast majority of the people they employ are volunteers. Add to this the fact that many governmental agencies also utilize volunteers and hundreds of corporations and churches are organizing intentional volunteer programs and you can see why volunteerism is still one of America's growth industries. We in this profession are responsible to see that it continues to thrive. It is essential for the health and well-being of our troubled communities.

Our "coming of age" period has taught us much, both about what works and what does not when involving volunteers in meeting community problems. We are now entering a period pregnant with possibilities for our experience to make the difference between success and failure as more and more needs begin coming back to states and communities to solve.

What we know and do has never been more important than at this very moment in history, for it will take the best and most creative thinking of staff, clients and volunteers to survive the next few years. Are we ready to re-commit to our unique paradigm of purpose?

As we share tools and techniques with you in these coming sessions, remember you are the experts where you are; remain open and flexible as you apply them. They must fit your reality to be useful. Also, as we look at possible creative new solutions to community problems, it is the volunteers who are most apt to come up with them. Why? Because they see our problems with "fresh eyes." They don't have the tunnel vision we so often get when living with problems eight to nine hours a day.

Two critical concepts for successful leadership are alternatives and options. We must always recognize there is never only one way to do anything. We must remain visionary enough to dream the *what ifs* and explore new avenues of delivering needed services.

Henry Ford once said, "Failure is the opportunity to begin again more intelligently." As challenging and disconcerting as exploring new frontiers of leadership and organizational change may be, it is critical that we become what I call "optimistic pragmatists," that is, informed but hopeful. One such leader today is Rosabeth Moss Kanter, the author of the highly respected book, *The Change Masters.*She observes that successful organizations of the future will embody the 5 Fs: *Fast, Focused, Flexible, Friendly,* and *Fun.*

There's a great story about Thomas Edison. A friend met him as he came out of his lab one night after working late on a project he had been immersed in for months with no success. The friend asked him "How many experiments have you done already?" "More than 1900," Edison replied. "That's incredible," replied his colleague, "You must feel very disappointed by now, very much a failure." Edison straightened up, his eyes glistening and said, "Not at all. I've made so much progress. You see, I now know more than 1900 things that won't work. One of these days I'm going to hit on the one that does."[3]

That's living with persistence and expectation!

To be the kind of leaders the field of volunteerism needs today requires more than just acquiring more management skills and techniques, as important as that may be. There are three distinct challenges before us:

- Knowing why we do what we do—our purpose as a profession
- Knowing where we are going—our vision for the field and our programs
- Knowing how to get there—our management expertise

What Do We Mean by Leadership?

For the past 30 years, I've been reading, writing, and pondering about the topic of leadership. The definition that captures the essence of what I want to suggest for leaders of volunteer programs comes from one of our own colleagues in this program, Mike Murray: "A leader is someone who dreams dreams and has visions and can communicate those to others in such a way that they, of their own free, will say yes!"

Let's examine the critical components of his definition for a moment. Having *dreams* and *visions* is not about where we are but where we want to be. That sounds so easy, logical and even fun, so why don't we do more of it in the field of volunteer administration? I would suggest it is because we are too busy doing, surviving, and coping. Who has time to dream except at 2:00 a.m.? Therefore, one of our biggest challenges is to shift our basic paradigm about how we *do* leadership (not how we talk about it). As you begin your journey as a volunteer manager, make dreaming a priority, not an afterthought! One of our CU program faculty members, John, shared this story at one of our training programs:

> On a flight to Chicago John happened to sit next to the head of the Planning Department for McDonald's fast food restaurants. John thought it was a great opportunity to pump the gentleman for information about how they did planning at McDonald's because it was such a hugely successful organization. The man told him that in their corporate headquarters there was a room on the top floor with nothing in it but a sky light and a water bed. Every key manager was required to spend an hour a week on that waterbed looking out the skylight and dreaming. As head of Planning, this executive spent an hour a day on the waterbed—it was part of his job description.

> Then he added that it was while he was on that waterbed it occurred to him how the trend of zero population growth would affect McDonald's. At the time McDonald's whole ad campaign revolved around kids and Ronald McDonald the clown. It was at that moment that the idea of McDonald's breakfast was born and marketing efforts were redirected towards baby boomers on their way to work.

I suggest the test of a good leader needs to stop being "how much have I done" and become "how many others have I involved?" This entails not doing all the work, but seeing that it is done and done well. This is an enormous and critical shift for volunteer administrators. It is the difference between being a *doer* and becoming a *leader.* When you master the skills of delegation and collaborative team building you will begin to have time to dream.

I always find the best way to start dreaming is to ask myself the question "What if . . .?" and let my imagination and energy combine to romp through the possibilities. For example, my current dream is: What if we truly learned to form and utilize collaborative, synergistic teams of volunteers and staff, between churches and agencies, among organizations and sectors in our communities? It boggles my mind what we could accomplish!

The other important concept in Murray's definition of leadership is to communicate your dream to others in such a way that they voluntarily and eagerly say yes! That sounds like volunteer recruitment, doesn't it?

Have you ever been motivated to action by a half-hearted, apologetic, tentative presentation? The clearer the vision and the more enthusiastically committed the leader is to it, the more likely it is that people will catch that vision. They have to see, feel, and experience the excitement and clearly understand how they can help make it happen. This is why a good organization mission statement is your most effective and compelling recruitment message. People want to make a difference, and they need to know what you are doing about a cause they can care about.

Warren Bennis once defined vision as "a target that beckons."[4] I have also heard it referred to as "a preferred future." It is that powerful and compelling dream about where we want to go that mobilizes people to help us get there. Every organization and every volunteer program needs a clearly articulated vision and it is the responsibility of leadership to provide it.

Let me share a story with you to illustrate this visionary leadership in action. It was in an issue of the United Airlines magazine, *Hemispheres.*

This story is about a man named Micky Weiss, who retired in 1987 after 40 years in the produce business in Los Angeles. Micky went to visit his son's produce firm in the Los Angeles wholesale market (a place he'd gone for 40 years) and was just in time to see a forklift hoist 200 flats of raspberries into a dumpster. This distressed fruit was still edible, but not marketable. All of the sudden a light bulb went on, an "a-ha" happened, a "what if..." occurred to him.

Six hundred people were going hungry in a tent city just five miles away, so he thought, "What if I found a way to get the wholesalers to stop dumping the produce and donate it to organizations that feed the hungry?" That day the Los Angeles charitable food distribution project was born. His produce colleagues caught the vision and were delighted with the idea. Student volunteers called agencies that got volunteers to pick up the fruit. By 1991, 1.5 million pounds of produce were being distributed to people who were hungry in Los Angeles.

He was joined by two University of Southern California professors involved in nutrition and public health. They heard about the project and shared their expertise to design a method to help share the program with other cities. As of 1995, it was in 27 cities and another 22 cities were developing it.

One person...one moment of "what if"...and the dream of feeding hundreds with nutritious food was realized. What are your *what ifs* for your program and/or for volunteerism?

Keeping Soul in our Work

Now let's talk for a moment about the concept of soul...and especially what it has to do with your work as volunteer managers. An amazing phenomenon has been occurring the past two to three years. The word "soul" is creeping into almost all the new leadership and management literature --and it is coming from the secular world. Whole books have been devoted to the topic, and others include chapters on it; many are ending up on the best-seller lists, including:

Care of the Soul by Thomas Moore
Leading with Soul by Lee Balman and Terrance Deal
The Heart Aroused by Stephen Whyte
The Art of Leadership by Max DePree
The Servant as Leader by Robert Greenleaf

I especially recommend an excellent collection of essays, entitled *Leadership in a New Era*, edited by John Renesch. It is one of the most thought-provoking books I have read in a long time. In one of the essays, there is this excellent illustration of the relationship of soul to work: "This was observed about Louis Armstrong... He is the greatest figure in the history of American jazz because he brought so much joy, happiness and love to people. There was no barrier between his horn and his soul."[5]

What a lovely tribute to a life! Perhaps one of our challenges is to examine honestly if there are barriers between our souls and our work that filter out our joy in serving. If so, what are they and how can we remove them?

I have realized that in those times that I have personally come close to burnout (when there seems to be more on my mind that there is room for and more to do than there is time for), I have been in grave danger of losing the soul in my work. It becomes just work. The passion, energy, dedication and excitement is crowded out and I find myself asking, "Is all this really worth it?" My joy diminishes and so does the quality of my work.

One thing that replenishes the "fire in the belly" for me is to revisit the vision and the purpose of what I believe volunteerism and volunteer leadership is all about. When I am clear about the *why* and infuse my work with heart and soul, I find people frequently commenting on how obvious it is that I love what I do. I am always somewhat taken aback when that happens and am tempted to respond "of course I love it, otherwise why would I be doing it?" There are many other things each of us could be doing and we also know we pay a price to work in this field (especially regarding salaries). So, are we crazy, or just not too bright?

Kathryn Graham once said, "To love what you do and feel that it matters—how could anything be more fun?" That is a gift beyond price. You are embarking on one of the most challenging and fulfilling jobs anyone could ever undertake—please don't ever forget that!

My goal is that you leave here not just equipped with the vital tools needed to ensure your competency but also with a clear, personal statement of vision and a commitment to invest your soul and spirit in the tremendously important work that you do. Wow! Is the world really ready for you?

---

[1] David Whyte, *The Heart Aroused* (Doubleday, 1994), 210.

[2] Peter Drucker, "It Profits Us to Strengthen the Non-profits." *The Wall Street Journal* (December, 1991).

[3] Rosabeth Moss Kanter, *The Change Masters* (Simon and Schuster, 1985), 65.

[4] Warren Bennis and Burt Nanus, *Leaders: Strategies for Taking Charge* (Harper & Row, 1985), 2-3.

[5] John Renesch, *Leadership in a New Era* (Cosimo Inc., 2002).

Section II: Our History—
Three Decades of Trends Affecting the
Profession of Volunteer Administration

Engraved above the entrance to the University of Colorado's Norlin library is a quote by former university president, George Norlin, "He who knows only his own generation remains always a child." These words remind me how important understanding the past is to informing the future.

I was blessed to become involved in the profession of volunteer administration in its infant years and have a front row seat during its exciting evolution. As a frequent keynote speaker for volunteer organizations from the 1970s to the 1990s, I spent a lot of my time thinking about emerging trends, and current issues. In 2008, it is unclear what will emerge as our new national professional association. I hope that, by sharing some of the history of volunteer administration, current and future leaders of the profession can learn and make more informed decisions about the future.

In this section, I share with you speeches from each of the decades that I think best illustrate the trends and issues of that moment. In revising them for this book, I feel satisfaction and wonder at our development, smile as I remember our groups being picketed and harassed, and also feel sadness that some issues have yet to be resolved, that in some things we haven't really come very far.

Colleagues pose for a photo op at an AVA conference.
Left to right: Joan Brown, Betty Stallings,
Jane Leighty Justis, Andy Hart, Jill Friedman Fixler,
Marlene, Jackie Norris, Trudy Seita

Breaking Down Academic Barriers

Conference of the American Association of Volunteer Services Coordinators,
the Association of Volunteer Bureaus
and the Association of Voluntary Action Scholars
Denver, CO, 1974

I have been asked to share with you the fascinating, sometimes frustrating experience of helping to convince a major university (namely the University of Colorado) that they should take the newly emerging profession of volunteer management seriously. It has been a three-and-a-half-year effort, but there have been three concrete and exciting results:

- The University of Colorado (CU) has sponsored three national workshops for volunteer administrators.
- CU's Department of Continuing Education now offers a nine-course interdisciplinary certification program for managers of volunteer programs. It is the first of its kind in the country, and it just won a national award from the National University Extension Association.
- Vicki Root has graduated from CU with a BA in Volunteer Administration through the Independent Study channel.

Those are the results. Now, let's trace back through those three-and-a-half years to see how they were brought about. Hopefully, some of our strategies and struggles may prove helpful to others of you who are engaged in the challenge of breaking down academic barriers that have traditionally plagued our profession.

First, let me digress. I just referred to volunteer administration as an emerging new profession. Some of you may say, "What do you mean, 'new'? Directors of volunteers have been around for a very long time."

That is true, so perhaps it would be more accurate to say it is an old profession in the process of re-discovering itself. I have had the opportunity of traveling to a number of parts of the country the past year training and talking to volunteer directors and wherever I go I find the same feeling of "a sleeping giant suddenly coming awake." These people are looking at their volunteer programs and communities and discovering three things:

1. They are in a highly competitive market for volunteers.
2. New programs are springing up to address new community needs (and old programs have to do some serious soul searching).
3. New kinds of people are volunteering (students, professional people, retired executives, blue-collar workers, etc.).

All of these things spell out the drastic need for new skills and new understandings to be able to direct viable, effective volunteer programs today. The 50-70 million volunteers are demanding it!

At this conference last year, Dr. Tessie Okin, professor at Temple University's School of Social Administration, made the challenge very clear when she said:

Modern volunteers are a unique breed whose ancestors helped build this country. Their potential is incalculable. Key persons on the American scene, closely involved with the volunteer citizen in action, are directors of volunteers, a group moving toward professionalization. The largest impact on masses of citizen volunteers may be had through appropriately training directors of volunteers.

And, it is that very subject we are here to talk about this morning.

I personally would rather be involved in the volunteer movement at this moment in history than at any other time. The challenges and needs are tremendous, sometimes overwhelming, but the interest is there to match it. I suspect we will continue to see progress made in this "professionalizing process" at an astounding rate in the next few years.

For us, the struggle began in November 1970 at a conference held in Boulder entitled College Curricula for Leadership of Human Service Volunteer Programs. This was sponsored by Dr. Ivan Scheier's National Information Center on Volunteers in Courts (NICOV; since changed to National Information Center on Volunteerism). The highlights of this conference included:

*   Forty-four conferees (24 from educational institutions, 17 from national or regional volunteer organizations, and 11 directors of volunteers) attended.

- The agenda was to discuss the kinds of colleges that might best respond to the needs of leaders of volunteer programs; what course content and curricula ought to be; and funding for such programs.
- Two distinct needs were identified:
  - Immediate, on-the-job training for leaders or directors of volunteer programs who were currently forced to "operate by the seat of their pants" (i.e., workshops and seminars).
  - Long-range development of an academic curriculum for volunteer administration, which would speak to the needs of present directors, but also prepare students to enter the field in the future.
- The consensus of this group was that "new schools, colleges, or departments did not need to be created, but new patterns needed to be used in existing schools and courses." This resulted from the shared observation that Volunteer Administration is truly inter-disciplinary in scope, and needs to embrace several fields (psychology, sociology, communications, business administration) while being owned by none of them.

One of the attendees at this conference was George Goulette, Director of Conferences and Institutes at CU. He became personally interested in the problem and held several meetings with Ivan and myself to explore what CU could and should be doing for this burgeoning new profession.

CU's Continuing Education Department was willing to experiment and test further the demand and their capability to meet it. We suggested they start with a three-day workshop for directors of volunteers in Colorado and surrounding states. This was held in February, 1972. It was co-sponsored by CU, NICOV and the Volunteer and Information Center (the Voluntary Action Center here in Boulder) which I direct. Harriet Naylor joined our efforts at that time as both staff and consultant. Her help proved to be invaluable. The response was most heartening, as 65 attended and indicated they were eager for more and longer training sessions.

Other national workshops were held at CU and co-sponsored by NICOV and the VIC:

- **July 1972:** A week-long skills workshop entitled "Directing Volunteer Programs" was held. At this workshop we cautiously began to incorporate management-oriented coursework (i.e., grantsmanship, decision making/problem solving, organizational climate and motivation) with the more traditional recruiting, interviewing, planning and evaluating sessions. Seventy-five attended this workshop representing 20 states, Canada and Africa. The evaluations indicated the group's mandate to pursue more management orientation in the future, as many directors had never been exposed to business courses before and recognized their need for management skills.

- **July 1973:** A week-long skills workshop entitled "Principles of Management Applied to Volunteer Administration" was held. The marriage between business management and volunteer administration was consciously made and incorporated throughout. We included two professors from the CU School of Business and Administration and an industrial management development consultant on the faculty.

  Courses were added such as "What Is a Manager?" "Motivation," "Achievement Motivation," and "Management by Objectives." We took the best and latest business had to offer, both in courses and people. We were working to offset negatives attitudes towards business. At this workshop, 100 people attended from 20 States and Canada. The conferees represented over 25 different types of volunteer programs. Evaluations were overwhelmingly in support of this marriage of management and volunteer administration and, they wanted more.

- **July 1974:** We are planning this workshop and it will continue using the same format as 1973. We will have faculty who are leaders in either volunteerism or business, academia and industry, emphasizing management by objectives, power and motivation, and the behavioral sciences.

As a result of this success, which we measured by the number of people attending and the feedback we received, we decided the time was ripe to get on with addressing the second need we had identified at the conference in February of 1972. That is, the development of a curriculum for volunteer administrators that would be available at and recognized by the university. A friend of mine said, "You can't just go on being a good egg, you either gotta hatch or go bad."

We recognized dual needs: to be interdisciplinary and to be available (beyond the Denver metro area) to those who could not invest two years to go back to college to get another academic degree. First, we pursued the idea of establishing an undergraduate degree program through the School of Business Administration. Problems arose in that there was no interest in a correspondence course through that route. Also, they were not open to flexibility of courses and we felt that was essential.

We shifted back to the Division of Continuing Education and they bought the idea immediately: a nine-course certification program for volunteer administrators. I am delighted to tell you it is available right now, for anyone,

The CU Team. Left to right: Top: Marlene and Jane Justis
Lower: Arlene Schindler, Betty Stallings, Mike King, and Elaine Yarbrough

anywhere in the U.S. who wants more training in this complex and fascinating field of ours.

Someone once observed that "nothing built ever arose to touch the skies unless someone dreamed that it could, someone believed that it should and someone willed that it must." I would submit that we in this room and at this conference are the ones who have been given the task to "will that it must."

Now that these courses are available, we must take the classes and encourage others to do so. We must also help design more programs, and not leave this up to academicians. We also need to come up with standardization so not just anything deserves a certificate. We must set and keep high standards. Last, we must work for the creation of an academic degree in this new profession.

Volunteerism
in Times of Change and Challenge

Association for Volunteer Administration National Conference
Seattle, WA, October 1985

I recently read this observation on progress by author Morris Mandel: "After several thousand years, we have advanced to the point where we bolt our doors and windows, and then turn on our burglar alarms—while the jungle natives sleep in open-doored huts."

Ironic, isn't it—what we call progress! So far, it has been difficult to find good news among all the headlines graphically reminding us of problems abroad and disaster at home. The encouraging word is becoming a rare and precious commodity.

When we consider the topic before us, it is apparent we're dealing with more than just a catchy, trendy title. I believe this issue is especially important to those of us in the field of volunteerism. The reason I say that is, I fear the most serious problem by far facing our country today is one of flagging spirits and fading optimism. Spirit and optimism have been unique hallmarks of this country from the beginning, and I agree with Eduard Lindeman, the pioneering social scientist in adult education and social philosophy, as to where this spirit has traditionally come from: "I wish I knew how to induce volunteers to appreciate the significant contributions they make to the democratic enterprise. They are to democracy what circulation of the blood is to the organism. They keep democracy alive."

So, you see why it's critical that those of us in volunteer leadership deal with this issue. If volunteers are indeed the unique nurturers of democracy, then we must help keep them alive and well. It just may mean the difference between preserving this country or not. For you all know, throughout our history, it's been volunteers with this voluntary spirit that have taken problems, turned them into challenges, and then set about finding answers to them. No human dilemma has been too awesome or overwhelming for them to tackle— education, health, disease of every kind, old age, poverty…the list is endless.

Ralph Waldo Emerson used to greet old friends with this question: "What has become clear to you since we last met?" Since there are so many dear friends in this assembly, I would like to share with you my answer to Emerson's question—what has become clear to me since we last met.

One thing that has become clear is that we are in the midst of a revolution. Within organizations, it is a revolution of followers and it has to do with how they have been led. It is a quiet revolution. They are not taking to the streets with placards and marches. They are finding subtle yet devastatingly effective ways to make their case:[1]

- Less than one in four jobholders is working at full potential.
- 75% of workers say they can be much more effective than they are.
- Productivity in this country has never been lower.
- More and more employees are doing their most creative things away from work (i.e., hobbies, avocations, etc.).

Why? In the book *Leaders* by Warren Bennis and Burt Nanus, the cause is identified clearly. "Leaders have failed to instill vision, meaning and trust in their followers." They go on to say. "We are approaching a major turning point in history where some new height of vision is sought, where some fundamental redefinitions are required, where tables of values have to be reviewed and measured in terms other than incomes, GNP and gas consumption."[2]

Those are pretty strong words, but there are books filling our bookstores right now that echo that theme. Just check them out next time you're in one:

Megatrends: Ten New Directions Transforming Our Lives, by John Naisbitt

In Search of Excellence, by Tom J. Peters and Robert H. Waterman

A Passion for Excellence by Tom J. Peters and Nancy K. Austin

The Change Masters by Rosabeth Moss Kanter

Further Up the Organization: How to Stop Management from Stifling People and Strangling Productivity by Robert Townsend

Leaders: The Strategies for Taking Charge by Warren Bennis and Burt Nanus

I think it is important for us to begin to deal honestly with this issue, for most of us are in both roles of followers and leaders. We report to someone and we have people who report to us.

What are our values and beliefs about leadership?

To check this out, I want to have you do a little fantasy exercise with me. Pretend you just received a new job. You will begin work on Monday and you will report to someone you have never worked for before. Think about this new manager for a moment. Now:

- List five words or phrases that describe what you hope this new manager will do or be.
- List five words or phrases that describe what you hope this person will not do or be.

Next, put yourself in the place of one of the people that works for you (a volunteer or paid staff person who presently reports to you). Look over the two lists you just made. Check those that describe how this person is experiencing your current leadership and management style. Be honest. What we want to get at is not how you *want* or *intend* to manage—but how you *do* it now.

The question we are struggling with is: Are your actions congruent with your beliefs about leadership? Your *actions* define your management style, not your words.

For 15 years, I have been writing and training in this field about the "enabler" style of management. I believe strongly in this style and have never had anyone disagree with the philosophy. It is right that we enable our volunteers and paid subordinates to be the best they can be. It is right that we care as much about our people as our programs. It is right that managers should be people growers. Is there anyone in this room that disagrees with those lofty ideals?

Then why do we keep being *doers* instead of *enablers*? I have seen little change of behavior in this profession in spite of a proliferation of training opportunities and books about it. People come (or stay home and read about it), listen, nod approval and then go home and keep on doing things the way they usually do until they drop or burn out or leave in utter frustration. It is a major concern of our profession and we must deal with it before it kills us...literally!

Our philosophy, words and actions must be congruent. When we believe certain things about leadership (i.e., it is right to enable others) but don't act on those beliefs, it creates dissonance within us, which creates internal stress, which leads to burn out. We know better but we don't act on it. As a farmer told a county agent who came to give him new information about seeds and planting, "I don't farm half as good as I know how already!" We, my friends, don't manage one half as well as we know how already.

We need to become more creative and flexible. How creative and flexible are we? That is an important question because, as we enter the 1980s, volunteerism is also in a tremendous state of flux. President Ronald Reagan declared in October 1981, "Volunteerism is an essential part of our plan to give government back to the people." Later in the speech he said, "Let us go forth and say to the people: Join us in helping Americans help each other."[3] And he proceeded to appoint a task force to encourage and initiate more voluntary effort nationally.

The clarion call has been picked up across the nation. For years we felt fortunate to get articles relating to volunteer efforts on the bottom of the women's section of our local newspapers. In the past few months, articles on volunteerism have appeared in *Time, Industry Week, The Christian Science Monitor, Business Week, Working Woman, The Wall Street Journal* and *Family Circle*.

This change is dramatic and more than a little overwhelming. Personally, it has caused me to feel like I have a split personality at times. On the one hand, I'm absolutely delighted that volunteers are at last being acknowledged and appreciated publicly and nationally. It's long overdue. And, the PR is also needed to recruit more citizens to become involved, something we desperately need; as *Time* pointed out, as of October 1, 1981, there are 100 million fewer federal dollars per day to spend on social programs and the arts. We need the help.

And, there is clear evidence that our people are both ready and willing to respond to worthwhile requests for help where they can make a difference. Daniel Yankelovitch, in his excellent book *New Rules: Searching for Self-fulfillment in a World Turned Upside Down*,[4] stated that many of the thousands of American adults he surveyed are longing for connectedness, commitment, and creative expression and that they expressed a poignant yearning to elevate the sacred and expressive side of life and diminish the impersonal, instrumental side that a technocratic society provides. What a magnificent match—volunteerism when done effectively provides just those things longed for: connectedness (with others who care about the same things), commitment (to a worthy cause), and creative expression (when volunteers' efforts are not misused or wasted).

But, the potentially negative side of this PR campaign is that there is too often a distinct naiveté regarding what it really takes to make volunteers' good intentions and efforts work effectively to meet needs. There is too often a cavalier notion that seems to imply: "Y'all come. As long as we mean well and you show up it's all going to work out okay."

Having invested the past 15 years working in this field, as a volunteer, Voluntary Action Center director, board member, consultant and author, I am convinced there could be nothing further from the truth. To make voluntary efforts work effectively in meeting needs like child abuse, day care, homemaking services, drug abuse, etc., it takes a partnership of trained professionals and volunteers.

Professional volunteer administrators today need not only to be skilled managers; they need to be skilled leaders. My colleague, Mike Murray, says: "A leader is someone who dreams dreams and has visions and can communicate those to other people in such a way that they say YES."

What dreams and visions do we have? Are we so busy coping that we've forgotten to have any? If so, we will rightfully have a hard time getting other people to say "yes" to what needs to be done.

We must avoid that subtle seducer "burnout"—especially as needs escalate and resources diminish. It is so tempting to try to be all things to all people. We end up working longer and longer, harder and harder, faster and faster. And, eventually we run out of steam. We must realize both our own potential and our limitations and not delude ourselves with a Messiah complex.

We need to replenish ourselves. Two areas of study I have found helpful here are stress and time management. John Gardner warns, "An individual cannot achieve renewal if he/she does not believe in the possibility of it, nor can a society." The key is to decide and act. It's critically important because, as a Nebraska friend once said, "You can't anymore give what you ain't got, than you can come back from where you ain't been."

Recognize when it's time to recycle the professional part of your life so that you're again learning and growing. But you won't have the time needed to recycle if you don't delegate. Doers burn out, delegators don't. That's the positive side of the changing, turbulent world in which we live. It provides endless opportunities for recycling to happen for everyone.

You may be tired or frustrated or discouraged enough at the moment that this sounds impossible. If so, remember Alice in Wonderland. One day she said to the Queen, "There's no use trying. One can't believe in impossible things!" The Queen smiled and replied, "I dare say you haven't had much practice. When I was your age, I always did it for a half hour a day. Why sometimes I've believed as many as six impossible things before breakfast!"[5]

Be careful about keeping an optimist with a sense of humor handy because negative people can pull you down. As a quadriplegic friend of mine says, "Never stumble on anything behind you."

I'd also like to say a word about performance. One of the diseases rampant in our society and organizations, in my opinion, is the mentality of mediocrity. It can be deadly to groups, organizations and persons. I once heard someone say: "It isn't necessarily the incompetent who destroy an organization. It's sometimes those who have achieved something and want to rest on those achievements."

Our national dilemma requires outstanding performance. *The Wall Street Journal* published an article in their January 1982 issue by psychologist Erik Larson, on the six characteristics of outstanding performers:

- They are able to transcend their previous levels of accomplishment (compete with themselves rather than others.)
- They avoid the so-called comfort zone otherwise known as a rut. (The only difference between a rut and a grave is how deep it is!)
- They are motivated by compelling internal goals.
- They solve problems rather than place blame.
- They confidently take calculated risks. Creativity is impossible without risk. Risk means we must be willing to fail and learn from the failure.
- They are able to rehearse coming actions and events mentally.

Some other observations Larson made: Outstanding performers are not workaholics; they take vacations and know when to stop working. They manage stress well and are masters of delegation so they don't get bogged down in detail. Strong performers have developed planning and organizational skills.

Do we have a "can do" attitude about our field? If not, why not? Let's look at the definition of some words for a moment:

Able: having power to do
Enable: to make able
Disable: to make unable or unfit, to cripple

As managers and leaders, we must face the reality that our style determines whether we enable or disable those who work with and for us.

Autocrats are managers who disable people with controlling top-down decision-making and manipulation. They decide and tell others what to do. They use this style out of a conviction or philosophy that this is what leaders should do.

Doers, on the other hand, disable people most often by default rather than by conviction. They mean to enable others, but they are so busy doing all the significant things themselves, that there is no time to teach, to mentor, to share their work or to listen.

The results are the same as far as the subordinate is concerned. That is the shocking truth we must face. We must make a conscious choice about what we—each of us—do to people.

So, we are all in it; the challenge is how will we respond?

There is a story about a physician named Dr. Henry Forbes—he had this vision of a long line of patients, streaming into his office all with the same problem. They all had sprained ankles from stepping into a deep hole right outside his office. His frustration was that he was so busy treating the ankles, he had no time to go fill in the hole.

Unfortunately this is a vivid description of how too many leaders / managers function much of the time. We're so busy treating symptoms, we rarely get at the cause of our problems.

For instance, take recruitment of volunteers. For those institutions that are still treating the problem as simply finding more traditional volunteers (like in the good old days)—they are missing the boat entirely. Erma Bombeck is quite clear about that:

> I cover the utility room beat. You cannot imagine the changes that have affected the American housewife during the last 10-15 years. She's down 1/4 of a child, works outside the home, her marriage made in heaven is virtually impossible to get parts for.

> The push buttons are fighting back. She's no longer being fulfilled by visiting her meat in the food locker and putting lids down.

> In fact, she is all but extinct. What has emerged is a brighter, more aware human being who does what she wants through choice.[6]

(And I might add, she has become very discriminating in what she is choosing to do as a volunteer!)

On the other hand, those agencies / organizations who have tried to examine the causes of the decreasing numbers of traditional volunteers see clearly why it's happened and know it will not only continue, but escalate in the 1980s.

In *The Statistical Abstract* of the U.S. for 1977, we discover why these changes are occurring:

- One in every three marriages in the U.S. ended in divorce in 1976 (the time of the last census). Now close to 1 in 2.
- There were three million more female heads of households in 1976 than in 1960 who were responsible for themselves and / or themselves and children.
- The number of working women nearly doubled between 1950-1976. (Another resource indicated that in 1979, 42.2% of the total U.S. work force was female and 49.4% of all married women worked outside the home.)
- The number of two-person households almost doubled between 1960-1976. This represented both young couples not having children and older couples living longer.
- The percentage of our population over 45 years of age was 31% in 1976. It is projected to be 42.5% by 2050.

I also read a *Denver Post* article stating that by the year 2000, one in every eight Americans will be over the age of 65. And, the fastest growing poverty group in the U.S. is single women over 50.

Dun's Review, May, 1979 added to these startling predictions:
- By 1985, there will be more divorces annually than first marriages.
- Almost one out of every three households will be headed by a single person by 1985.
- By 1990 women will account for 45% of those employed.
- By 1990 only 1/2 of the nation's children will live with both parents (2 out of 3 do today).

There have also been drastic changes in the makeup of the paid workforce during the 1970s and 1980s which undoubtedly impact the *volunteer* workforce.
- 41-45% male (many seeking service/client related work).
- Fewer traditional non-working, housewife volunteers. More women seeking administrative/decision-making jobs.
- Fastest growing segment of volunteer workforce is working people.
- Between 1975-1990 there was a 55% increase in people between the ages of 25-44 in the paid workforce.
- In addition, a 6% decrease in workers age 16-24 between1980-85.
- Specifically for volunteers the time period saw:
  - Corporate interest in hiring paid volunteer coordinators.
  - Need for shorter, project-oriented assignments. Assignments need to not be open-ended.
  - Hours of availability: after 5pm and on the weekends.
  - Must be organized for busy people!

There is opportunity for new skills and professional know-how, but we have to help volunteer leaders understand and not be threatened.

- Youth: Career exploration and resume building opportunity through volunteerism.
- Seniors: Retire earlier, with more skills
- Self-Help/neighborhood groups
- Young couples delaying childbirth: "Borrow" them to work with your kids as practice!

Have you changed/updated your volunteer recruitment in light of these trends? We also must heed the trends that are affecting the work place because most of our organizations have paid employees, many of you are paid staff, and working people are now the fastest growing segments of the volunteer work force nationally.

Five Major Shifts that Will Affect Volunteering

The statistics below came from *U.S. Abstract of the Census* (referred to previously) and *Dun's Review* 1979.

Shift #1: The Coming Shortage of Youth. Because of the low birth rate of the 1960s, the number of young workers will drop sharply in the 80s. The 16-24 year old group of workers will decline 6% or 2.8 million youth from 1980 to 1985.

Shift #2: The Middle-Age Bulge. There will be an amazing demographic bunching up of the 25-44 age workers in the 1980s. In 1975, there were 39 million workers in this age bracket, and by 1990 there will be 60.5 million, an extraordinary jump of 55%. They will comprise 52% of the total work force. This would lead the experts to anticipate intense competition for promotion and severe disappointments due to limited opportunities for upward mobility. Some of the major personnel and management problems of the eighties will revolve around this critical group in the work force.

Shift 3: The Expanding Role of Women. The participation of women in the workforce is expected to increase until, by 1990, 61% of all American women will be working for pay, outside their homes.

Shift #4: Competition for Desirable Jobs. The rise in the number of qualified minority and female workers will add to the competition referred to in Shift #2.

Shift #5: Increased Employment of Older Workers. American retirement patterns are changing primarily due to the extension of mandatory retirement to age 70, the increasing number of older persons and the effects of double-digit inflation.

We must be first in line to study the results of the 1980 census—so we can understand the newest demographics and use this knowledge to plan realistically for the future.

The needs of the team are best met when we meet the needs of individual persons. By conceiving a vision and pursuing it together, we can solve our problems of effectiveness and productivity, and we may at the same time fundamentally alter the concept of work. —Max DePree

---

[1] In preparing for this presentation, I used many different sources and do not have specific citations for all the data used.

[2] Warren Bennis and Burt Nanus, *Leaders: Strategies for Taking Charge* (Harper & Row, 1985), 8.

[3] Ronald Reagan, *Remarks at the Annual Meeting of the National Alliance of Business* (October 5, 1981). Speech presented at Sheraton Washington Hotel. Accessed http://www.reagan.utexas.edu/archives/speeches/1987/091487d.htm.

[4] Daniel Yankelovitch, *New Rules: Searching for Self-fulfillment in a World Turned Upside Down* (New York: Random House, 1981).

[5] Lewis Carroll and Martin Gardner, *The Annotated Alice: Alice's Adventures in Wonderland & Through the Looking Glass* (New York: C.N. Potter, 1960).

[6] Erma Bombeck. Source unknown.

Our Profession at a Crossroads

Keynote at the International Conference on Volunteer Administration
Atlanta, GA, October 1991

"Today, loving change, tumult, even chaos is a prerequisite for survival, let alone success."[1] This rather startling statement was made by Tom Peters, in his book *Thriving on Chaos*. He goes on in that same book to warn that constant change requires that we dramatically increase our capacity to accept disruption.

Robert Fulghum, in his book, *Uh-Oh*, uses his wonderful sense of humor to illustrate the same point:

"Uh-oh"…is a frame of mind. A philosophy.

It says to expect the unexpected, and also expect to be able to deal with it as it happens most of the time. "Uh-oh" people seem not only to expect surprise, but they count on it, as if surprise were a dimension of vitality.

"Uh-oh" embraces "here we go again" and "now what" and "you never can tell what's going to happen next" and "so much for a plan A" and "hang on, we're coming to a tunnel" and "no sweat" and "tomorrow's another day" and "you can't unscramble an egg" and "a hundred years from now it won't make any difference."

"Uh-oh" is more than a momentary reaction to small problems. "Uh-oh" is an attitude—a perspective on the universe. It is part of an equation that summarizes my view of the conditions of existence:

$$Uh\text{-}huh + oh\text{-}wow + uh\text{-}oh + oh, God = Ah\text{-}hah!$$ [2]

If these statements are true, and I believe they are, it may help explain why it's very likely that almost everyone in this audience has been to a workshop or seminar, read a book or heard a speech during the past year that had one of the following as a major theme:

- Managing change effectively
- Moving into the new century
- Living creatively in a changing world
- Paradigm shifts

This is not only appropriate, but necessary for our personal and professional growth and sanity since we are living at a time when all aspects of life for persons, organizations, and society as a whole are changing more rapidly and dramatically than at any other time in the history of the world. And, it's all happening simultaneously. It's no wonder we feel overwhelmed much of the time.

It is at this very point of great need, to understand this new world and acquire new skills to deal with it, that I would issue a word of caution. Let's not fall into that well-known American trap—the quick fix. All you have to do is walk into any bookstore and the shelves are bulging with how-to manuals filled with jargon and simple formulas guaranteed to make us instant experts at managing change.

The reality is change is hard. Carl Sandberg once observed, "Life is like an onion. You peel it off one layer at a time and sometimes you weep." Change does include, by necessity, disruptions, death of what has been and therefore grieving. It's vital that we not trivialize or romanticize it. Probably the reality for most of us is more apt to be what one sage observed, "No one likes change but a wet baby."

How can we move from dreading change to liking it, or at least dealing creatively with it? The first step, in my opinion, is recognizing that although change is indeed hard, it can also provide opportunities for enormous hopefulness and growth. Gail Sheehy writes, in her book, *Passages:*

> *With each passage from one stage of human growth to the next, we, too, must shed a protective structure. We are left exposed and vulnerable—but also yeasty and embryonic again, capable of stretching in ways we hadn't known before.*[3]

May we in this profession join the ranks of the new breed of leaders that Stephen Covey speaks about in his widely respected book, *The Seven Habits of Highly Effective People.* He talks about leaders today seeking "deeper, more substantive solutions—they are tired of glitzy quick fixes and superficial answers."[4] Instead, they want to solve the chronic underlying problems and focus on the principles that bring long-term results.

And so, we come to one of the major crossroads for this profession of volunteer administration. I believe that we must be willing to move beyond information and even knowledge, into wisdom. We have been engaged in the vital process of establishing and defining this profession for the past thirty years. We are young in terms of being a profession and have had to invest enormous energy in these necessary developmental tasks. I'm sure it is hard for those of you who have been volunteer administrators for less than 10-15 years to realize how far we've come in such a relatively short time.

Since I'm one of the oldest tribal storytellers still around in our profession, let me share a bit of our history with the newcomers. It's especially important today, when we face the challenge of some large and glitzy campaigns that seem to indicate that volunteerism has just been discovered, that it's a new phenomenon.

So, let me share some of our milestones.

Founding

The Association for Volunteer Administration (AVA) was founded 30 years ago by Miriam Karlins and first was called American Association of Volunteer Services Coordinators (AAVSC). It was primarily made up of volunteer coordinators in mental health and hospitals, because these were the only organizations to have them. In 1971, the organization opened up to volunteer administrators from all types of agencies and organizations. Now we have 1800 members in AVA and literally thousands of other volunteer directors and coordinators who have not joined our association. To estimate the number is impossible for there are now 489,882 charitable organizations listed by the IRS and there are also volunteer directors in governmental agencies and corporations. The numbers are indeed staggering.

Status

During the past 20 years, this profession has not only grown in size but in status. Our goal has been to be professional in what we do and slowly, the job descriptions, salaries and status of our members are beginning to reflect this.

An example of how far we've come: in 1970 the Census Bureau and Department of Labor classified our work in the "miscellaneous clerical" category. Thanks to the monumental efforts of Harriet Naylor, one of our founding matriarchs and mentor to many, we are now recognized as professionals by those entities.

Regarding the status of our field, Rodney Dangerfield could have been our spokesperson because "we got no respect"! A story I remember that sums it up best was an incident at a conference held at the University of Michigan in the mid-1970s. It was sponsored by Harriet Naylor and National Center for Voluntary Action on the topic of education for volunteer administrators. We were picketed by a carpenter's union and we had to break through the line to get to the assembly hall. We were called "scabs" and several other choice epitaphs. It was extremely upsetting to us "nice folks who just like to help others." The picketers marched into the hall and took over the microphone. We sat there horrified.

It seems that some volunteers had helped build homes for elderly people in Florida and these carpenters claimed that volunteers took jobs away from people. That is why they were picketing. Finally, a hand went up from the audience and a young woman asked if they were open to questions. When the spokesperson said "yes," the young woman said, "Are all of you who came here tonight being paid to do this?" The answer was, "Of course not!" "Then," she said, "*You* are all volunteers. You happen to volunteer for a cause you believe in, and so do we." With that the picketers laid down the microphone and quietly left. That person was Energize, Inc. President Susan J. Ellis, then a new volunteer program manager for the Philadelphia Family Court.

During that same time period, I was picketed and heckled by women's liberation groups. The leaders of women's liberation had taken a national stance against volunteerism saying it "exploited women." This stance was later reversed and they ended up staffing their whole national office with volunteers. Things were definitely never boring in those days.

So you see, you are in a field that has come an incredibly long way in less than 20 years. What fun it has been to have experienced and been a part of these changes.

Literature

The first book for our field was written in 1967 by Harriet Naylor, *Volunteers Today: Finding, Training and Working with Them*. In the early 1970s, Ivan Scheier wrote two books about volunteers in court settings and Eva Schindler-Rainman and Ron Lippitt wrote *The Volunteer Community*. In 1976, I wrote my first book, *The Effective Management of Volunteer Programs*, which I self-published because the publishing houses I approached said there was no identifiable market for it. How wrong they were, for *The Effective Management of Volunteer Programs* has sold over 100,000 copies. For the first ten years of this field, you could carry the entire library of volunteer management literature in one small briefcase.

Where are we now? Have you checked out our resource room? We have entire catalogs full of our own literature (books, magazines, newsletters written by and for our profession). This is one of the criteria for being a profession and we have met it well. We still need more books, especially those that will take us *beyond* the how-tos.

Training and Education

Before 1972, there was no generic training available in this field. A few large voluntary organizations such as the American Red Cross, Girl Scouts and Junior League had training but it was for their own constituents. In 1972, Ivan Scheier and I worked to begin the University of Colorado's Volunteer

Management Certificate Program. It has been 20 years in the running and we estimate over 3000 volunteer administrators have been through the program.

Where are we now? There are literally hundreds of events held every year at local, state, provincial and national levels to learn the competencies of our profession. The problem has become choosing the event that fits your needs and budget. What a nice problem to have. And, we are keeping up with this wonderful age of technology by offering training by audio and video tapes. Another important development is that AVA provides a certification process to verify when we have acquired those competencies that make us truly professional.[5]

Marlene training in the early '80s.

Yes, the work of these past 20-30 years has been necessary, important and well done. We now have access to the information, knowledge, tools and techniques needed by our profession and we should celebrate that accomplishment together.

Today's Crossroads

This is the road that has led us to this place and this time in our history. Now we are at the crossroads I mentioned earlier. Are we willing and ready to begin to move beyond just more information and knowledge and into wisdom?

It would seem clear it is not a choice of either/or but a need for both that will help our profession choose that fork in the road that will allow us to be viable and valuable in a changing world. It will help us move out of the developmental stage of an emerging profession and into the influential stage of a maturing profession.

Robert Frost, in his classic poem, "The Road Not Taken," depicts the challenge so poignantly:

Two roads diverged in a yellow wood,
And sorry I could not travel both
And being one traveler, long I stood
And looked down one as far as I could
To where it bent in the undergrowth;

Then took the other just as fair,
And having perhaps the better claim,
Because it was grassy and wanted wear;
Though as for that the passing there
Had worn them really about the same,

And both that morning equally lay
In leaves no step had trodden black.
Oh, I kept the first for another day!
Yet knowing how way leads on to way,
I doubted if I should ever come back.
I shall be telling this with a sigh
Somewhere ages and ages hence:
Two roads diverged in a wood, and I—
I took the one less traveled by,
And that has made all the difference.[6]

One important question for us to ask at this crossroads is, "What should our unique contribution be?" What is the unique calling we've said "yes" to in this profession? I think Harriet Naylor said it best in a speech she made to this very group in 1974: "If doctors are concerned with health and lawyers with justice as their ideal, then I believe our profession is concerned with freedom of choice...I believe freedom is our responsibility."

This is what I mean by wisdom, knowing the *why* behind all we do. Is this still what we believe our profession is about—being the guardians of democracy and free choice for all people? Will we protect and extend the precious right of service to all our citizens regardless of race, age, sex or religious beliefs? If so, we have a contribution to make not only to this country but to all the emerging democracies around the world.

If we take the other fork in the road that we could so easily take, that is, maintaining what we have gained, or continuing to just get better at doing the same things, or concentrating on knowledge at the expense of wisdom, then in my opinion, we are in deep jeopardy.

Max DePree talks about the trap of "entropy" into which any organization can fall. He says everything has a tendency to deteriorate. He's simply referring to the danger of getting into ruts. We are passing through the critical "middle-aged" slump in this profession. It's at this stage it would be far too easy to become settled and satisfied. In *Passages*, Gail Sheehy has this to say about middle age:

> *If we confront ourselves in the middle passage and find a renewal of purpose around which we are eager to build—this might well be the best years, but if one has refused to bridge through midlife transition then the sense of staleness will calcify into resignation.*[7]

This is important for us as persons as well as organizations. Stephen Covey recommends we each do our own life mission statements at least every decade (not goals and objectives, but *mission*): what is our reason for being? I just celebrated my 60th birthday and the 15th anniversary of my company, Volunteer Management Associates. These milestones made this seem like an appropriate time for me to re-examine my own life mission. Here is what I came up with for me as I've determined to avoid the trap of entropy as a person.

- To say centered. To do that I must remember my center is my spiritual life. My challenge is to keep experiencing God as mystery and never try to shrink God to fit my own limitations. I want to keep questioning and exploring as long as I live.
- To keep learning, growing and changing in all aspects of my life. To stop growing is to die!
- To be joyful and thankful for the incredible gifts of life, large and small, and to share that joy.
- To value relationships with my family and friends above all else.
- To be doing work that I love and that matters, both to me and others. It must contribute to the healing and well-being of the world in some way.
- To play more and let my over-disciplined child within free to romp in this new period of my life.
- To value and treasure all my past roles in life and to be open and willing to risk possible new roles, especially that of "crone-in-training."

Perhaps I'd better pause and say a word about what I mean by a "crone." What I don't mean is Webster's definition: "A withered, witchlike old lady." What I do mean is the concept of crone that comes from mythology and Jungian psychology, "the truth teller at the crossroads;" the wise woman who has gone through her many crossroads of life and has reached a place of conscious surrender where her ego demands are no longer relevant. She is not indifferent or withdrawn but is totally present. She can be who she is and live her naked truth and is therefore like a tuning fork in her environment.

So, being a "crone-in-training" seems like a worthwhile goal at my age and stage of life. It should keep me challenged for the rest of my life!

Another crossroad for our profession, I'd like to suggest, has to do with determining if, in fact, it is time for us to consider some basic paradigm shifts. Let's spend a few moments examining what that means. I've learned, whenever any new term becomes accepted jargon, it's easy but often false to assume we all know what the term means.

Here are some definitions of the word "paradigm":

- The lens through which we see the world.
- Our perceptual map of reality.
- The belief system into which we fit our experiences. It filters our incoming data. (I wouldn't have seen it if I hadn't believed it.") We often distort data to fit our own paradigms.

May I suggest a few paradigm shifts for us to consider in this profession?

From this...	To this...
From connectors of needs and resources...	To guardians of free choice and freedom.
From administrators...	To: • Enablers of citizen participation • Community resource mobilizers • America's talent scouts
From reactive, low-power profession...	To proactive, highly influential profession.
From transfusion technicians providing new blood (volunteers) to ailing agencies...	To surgeons specializing in heart transplants.
From the attitude that volunteer administration is a dead-end job...	To a career becoming ever more essential to nations in distress.
From maintaining the status quo...	To becoming "creativity consultants" seeking out those volunteers who can bring in new solutions to the enormous problems our communities face.
From "lone rangers" and the most dedicated "doers" in the world...	To collaborative team-building experts in our own departments, organizations and our communities.
From comforting the afflicted...	To also afflicting the comfortable when necessary.

As you can see, we have not one choice at this crossroads but many. Sheehy tells us, "More than anything else, it is our own view of ourselves that determines the richness or paucity of the middle years."[8]

May I close with an observation and a challenge?

Observation: There are indeed many paradigms to choose from and for most of us it will be a combination of several. We must remember how important those choices are for each one of us, for the lens through which we see our profession will determine how others see us.

Challenge: It is my honest conviction that never before have our organizations, our communities and our nation needed what we do and what we know more desperately. And, never before have we been as well prepared to deliver it.

We stand at the foot of an awesome mountain and there are three paths to choose from:

1. To return back down the long and difficult, but safe and familiar path that brought us here.
2. To take the path that circles the mountain but never gets us to the top.
3. To check our gear, add some high altitude equipment and new mountain climbing skills, renew our energy and begin to scale the mountain before us, tackling the greatest challenge we've faced yet.

Which will it be? The choice is ours and the time is now.

---

[1] Tom Peters, *Thriving on Chaos* (Alfred Knopf, 1987), 45.

[2] Robert Fulghum, *Uh-Oh* (Villard Books, 1991).

[3] Gail Sheehy, *Passages* (E.P. Dutton, 1953), 20.

[4] Stephen Covey, *The Seven Habits of Highly Effective People* (Free Press, 1989), 40, 42.

[5] As of 2008, Certification in Volunteer Administration is offered by the Council for Certification in Volunteer Administration. See http://www.cvacert.org/index.htm.

[6] Robert Frost, "The Road Less Taken," in *Mountain Interval* (H. Holt and company, 1916).

[7] Sheehy, op. cit., 31.

[8] Sheehy, 345.

Listening to Today—
Envisioning Tomorrow

International Conference on Volunteer Administration
Dallas, TX, October 1998

I am truly thrilled and delighted to be in this place, at this time, with this incredible group of colleagues and friends. I know every speaker is supposed to say something like that but I have never meant it more deeply than at this moment. For those of you who may not know, I had a stroke in May and there were quite honestly times during these past five months when I was not sure if this would be possible. But thanks to the grace of God, incredible loving care of friends and family (many of you in this room), excellent medical attention, unrelenting nagging by physical therapists and well-meaning friends, plus a stubborn Viking spirit—here I am.

I am eager to share the next hour with you as we explore together the issues and challenges of today and my vision for the future.

As I have been immersed in reading your e-mails and catching up on that inevitable stack of articles and books in the process of preparing for these remarks, one book review caught my eye especially. Actually, it was the title. The book was called *Blur,* and it was written by futurists Stan Davies and Christopher Meyer and they point out the blurring of so many of the "givens" we in our society have traditionally had; for example:

Products are services—buyers are sellers—homes are offices—workers are capitalists. The line between structure and process, owning and using, knowing and learning is dissolving. The pace is furious, the meltdown so severe, the erasing of borders so complete, that the whole picture is going out of focus—it's a blur.[1]

The authors use a powerful analogy, that it's like either being in or standing and watching a bullet train speed by. It's amazing, efficient and very disorienting.

As I thought about that bullet train image of change, I was reminded of one of my favorite stories. It's about a nurse walking a mental patient on the grounds of the hospital. A pigeon flew overhead and did what pigeons frequently do. The droppings landed on the head of the patient. The nurse got very shook up and said, "Stay right there, John. Don't move. I'm going to run back and get some toilet tissue, I'll be right back." John replied calmly, "Don't worry about it nurse. That bird is going to be long gone by the time you get back."

So, in sorting through the blur of issues we could possibly consider and to help us focus on those that will be there when we get back, I'm going to have you disembark from the bullet train for awhile and join me in another mode of transportation. We're going to parasail instead.

My husband, Harvey, and I were in Greece and while sunning on the beach, we watched people parasailing over a lake. We finally got up nerve enough to try it and what an incredible experience! The most amazing thing was how my perspective changed as I viewed the scenery, calmly floating far above everything. I could even see Albania across the water. So ever since that time, when I face a big problem or confusing set of issues, I try to mentally parasail.

By parasailing together, I hope we can achieve several things:
• Stop feeling frantic and enjoy the ride.
• Gain perspective regarding the issues of our profession as they interrelate to one another and to the mega-issues of the world at large; hunger, housing, health, environment.
• Be more able to live and work "with a deep appreciation for the past, an enriched sense of the present and a joyous anticipation for the future."[2]

I am going to concentrate on five umbrella issues:
• Diversity
• Technology
• Funding
• Risk management
• Our role as leaders

Then I'd like to end with a vision for the future. As we delve into each of these, I ask you to ponder two things:

1. Are we asking the right questions? Anthony Jay said, "A non-creative mind can spot wrong answers, but it takes a creative mind to spot wrong questions."
2. What are the paradoxes within these issues?

Issue 1: Diversity

For as long as I've been in this field, when the issue of diversity has been discussed, the question has usually been stated like this:

How can we recruit more ethnic minority volunteers and volunteer directors?

As you can see by looking around the room, we have still not been very successful in dealing with that challenge.

I would like to suggest that this is the wrong question in many communities where you serve. And, by the end of the first decade of the new century, it will be the wrong question for us nationally because white Americans are rapidly becoming the minority (and we are very good at recruiting them). So, the new question becomes...

How can we recruit more of the majority of Americans to become volunteers and volunteer directors?

Think about that as it relates to the future of volunteerism and our field and the issue moves up from the back burner very quickly.

The whole meaning and challenge of diversity has exploded into something much larger and complex than we traditionally viewed it. I receive more e-mails relating to this issue than any other. It's the topic of dozens of articles and debated not just here, but in global forums as well.

I would ask you to revisit the image of the blurring of societal boundaries portrayed by Davies and Meyer and apply that to our own field. What are a few of those blurred boundaries that are greatly impacting what we do and how and why?

Clients are volunteers—volunteerism is being mandated—employed people make up the majority of the volunteer workforce—some volunteers are paid. There is now no "traditional" volunteer—remember the days of the "little old lady in tennis shoes" and Junior League matrons? Today we have five generations of volunteers working simultaneously, often in the same programs.

One of my correspondents suggested, "It's time to blast the lid off many of our assumptions and stereotypes." I would like to consider three assumptions.

Assumption #1: There are three distinct and separate sectors in democratic societies: the public (government), the private (for-profit) and the voluntary (not-for-profit).

Viewing this from our parasail, we can see that in volunteerism, the boundaries between these sectors have not only blurred, but almost disappeared. For example:

- **The government** has established thriving volunteer programs at local, county, state and national levels. They also legislated and funded programs of national service (AmeriCorps, Senior Corps, Learn and Serve, etc.). In many other countries (Britain, Canada, Poland), government has been the primary funder of most voluntary efforts.
- **Corporations** have hired directors of volunteers, instituted release time for employee volunteering and made a strong commitment to corporate social responsibility (thanks in large part to the efforts of the Points of Light Foundation).
- **The voluntary sector** has been expected to assume responsibility for many of the programs once considered the government's responsibility, but which have been diminished or dropped due to funding cutbacks. We've also been given the challenge of helping to make new government initiatives like Welfare-to-Work succeed.

The paradox is that in the midst of the confusion, and at times, chaos, of these now blended sectors, there has never been a greater opportunity for meaningful collaboration. We need one another in increasingly significant ways.

Assumption #2: Volunteerism is a uniquely American phenomenon.

Here are the realities:

- Since 1970, an organization called the International Association for Volunteer Efforts (IAVE) has held biennial worldwide conferences. Just since 1990 these have been held on five continents (France, Argentina, South Africa, Japan and this year it was held in Alberta, Canada with 2900 volunteer leaders from 90 nations participating).
- For more than ten years, a group founded by Elizabeth Hoodless, from England, has been conducting conferences for volunteer leaders in European and North African communities.
- Thirteen Eastern European countries are in the process of establishing volunteer centers and Poland already has several. And this despite the astounding fact that less than a decade ago all were behind the Iron Curtain.
- We're delighted that every year at this conference we have more and more of our attendees from other countries. We look forward to that trend continuing in the future.
- The United Nations has declared 2001 as the International Year of Volunteers.

Global boundaries have blurred and what an exciting and enriching opportunity that is for all of us.

Assumption #3: There is a common understanding and acceptance of the definition of the word "volunteer."

The traditional definition, as stated in the excellent book, *By the People* by Susan J. Ellis and Katherine H. Campbell, has been:

> *To volunteer is to choose to act in recognition of a need, with an attitude of social responsibility and without concern for monetary profit, going beyond one's basic obligations.*[3]

The key elements are:

- Free choice
- Social responsibility (benefiting others)
- Without personal economic gain

That's the definition of the word, but there's a more esoteric aspect of volunteerism that is difficult to define. You have to experience it. It is the wondrous phenomenon of people helping people, often with anonymous acts of kindness that ennoble the human spirit. At its best, volunteerism creates hope in the hearts of the receivers and meaning and purpose in the lives of the givers. The end result is a more caring and civil society.

Volunteerism is love made visible and it changes lives, changes communities and can change the world. And this, my dear friends, is what keeps us doing *what* we're doing and loving it passionately!

The challenge that has emerged as one of the most critical we face in this profession is not about the phenomenon of volunteerism, but about the semantics and statistics we use in interpreting its many iterations to the world. Why has this problem occurred? Again, it relates to the problem of blurring!

- The enormous influx of **mandated**, court-referred volunteers. How can you "mandate" volunteerism?
- The movement of **requiring** students to volunteer in order to meet graduation requirements.
- The increase in **stipends** for volunteers and the question it raises— at what point does this crossover from enabling funds to becoming economic gain?
- The increased emphasis on **citizen participation** or citizen involvement (i.e., America's Promise).
- The expectation that managing all of these forms of "free" service should be enfolded into the job description of the director of volunteers and reported under the one heading of "volunteers" in our statistics.

Sarah Jane Rehnborg (Association for Volunteer Administration past president and associate director of the RGK Center for Philanthropy and

Community Service at the University of Texas) issues the challenge in powerful and compelling terms in a recent article entitled, "The Limits of the 'V' Word."

Are we helping ourselves by continually trying to group everything that happens in our field under the label "volunteer"? We are selling ourselves short by not clarifying our language and by lumping all manners and forms of service within one broad and reasonably useless classification of "volunteer." [4]

And so, some of the questions I would suggest we seriously ponder, debate and decide about are:

- How do we acknowledge, encourage and support the important movements of citizen participation and still maintain the integrity of the philosophy of volunteerism (free choice and without economic gain)?
- Is it time to advocate for a change of title, from director or coordinator of volunteers to director of volunteers and citizen participation, citizen involvement or community service?
- How do we record and report on the two as separate but equal, so we and others can understand the difference?

I suggest this be a major project for AVA during the next year so we can have the clarification and definition come from this professional association concerned solely with volunteerism. It deserves our best attention.

Finally, in looking at our challenges as we consider this broad and increasingly complex issue of diversity, I am reminded of the dilemma of deciding whether to become specialists or generalists as defined by one sage:

A specialist is someone who knows more and more about less and less, until they know practically everything about almost nothing.

A generalist is someone who knows less and less about more and more until they know almost nothing about everything.

Versatility and flexibility are the keys and the view from our parasail suggests we have never before in history had a richer, more extravagantly luxuriant variety of cultures, talents, ages, professional skills and opportunities to truly make a difference in this field called volunteerism.

Issue 2: Technology

Not too long ago, I remember the chief concern of volunteer directors regarding technology was "How can I get my agency to get the volunteer department its own computer?" Then it became, "How can we get a computer that is not donated and out-of-date?" Now our field is right smack in the middle of the technological revolution that is impacting all the rest of society. It's a whole new ballgame, and it's affecting every aspect of what we do:

- **Records and systems.** Dozens of computer programs are now available to help us become more efficient in this important area.
- **Communication**
  - The newsletter *Grapevine* lists over 500 Web sites containing information and services regarding volunteerism.
  - The Internet, e-mail and faxes have given us "the world on a keyboard" as so eloquently stated by Susan Ellis.
- **Recruitment,** especially recruiting on the Web.
- **Virtual volunteering:** one of the hottest things going. Volunteer from your computer and never leave home. A recent workshop sponsored by New York AVA was entitled, "Hook 'em through the Internet."
- **Education/Training.** Our own professional development and training for volunteers and staff:
  - Energize, Inc., Susan Ellis' company and Web site, completely devoted to providing training materials, information and resources for volunteer management professionals.
  - Online courses, such as the one at Washington State University developed by Nancy McDuff.
  - Interactive videos
  - Distance learning (Points of Light series of self-study courses; the Norwich University Center for Volunteer Administration in Vermont has had correspondence courses for several years thanks to Carol Todd.)
  - Courses on diskettes: Betty Stallings' *Training Busy Staff to Succeed with Volunteers: The 55-Minute Staff Training Series*, offered as hard copy and on diskette.[5]
  - Entire courses on video from The University of Colorado Volunteer Management Certificate Program that can be viewed from home. To do this in person would require three weeks and three trips to Colorado.[6]

As I researched all of these new avenues of incredible possibilities on the information superhighway, I was reminded of a quote from Will Rogers commenting years ago on the transportation revolution in this country: "The trouble with American transportation is that you can get somewhere quicker than you can think of a reason for going there."[7]

So, may I suggest just a few cautionary questions for us to ponder as we explore and master these technological wonders?

How do we insure that we utilize technology as another valuable means to an end, like the other tools and techniques we've developed to help us achieve our mission of serving people and enriching and improving society?

We must never get so enamored with the machines that we neglect the people, for we are in the people business, first and foremost! An example of technology gone amuck in my opinion: I recently read about an organization in Los Angles that operates a telephone service that gives callers an opportunity to confess their wrongs to an answering machine. They get 200 callers each day leaving one-minute messages. My imagination then completes this scenario like this: "When finished press 3" and a message comes on saying, "Hey, dude, remember, I'm OK, you're OK, we're all OK, have a nice day."

How do we become increasingly skilled and discriminating Web surfers? I think of surfers on the ocean. The best ones learn quickly which waves to let go by and do nothing about and which waves to catch that will take them right into shore, which is where they want to go.

How do we insure that we never allow convenience to replace commitment in virtual volunteering and Internet recruiting? That the matching of right volunteers to right jobs must remain primary and the technique to do so is still skilled and professional interviewing. I am so pleased that Jayne Cravens and other leaders of the virtual volunteering project[8] are strongly emphasizing "a well-organized agency and volunteer program are key elements to virtual volunteering success."

Are we willing and ready in this profession to begin to move beyond just more information and knowledge into wisdom? I asked this question in an AVA keynote address six years ago and I think it's even more pertinent today. It would seem clear it is not a choice of either/or but a need for both that will help our profession be viable and valuable in a changing world. It will help us move out of the developmental stage of an emerging profession into the influential stage of a maturing profession.

Issue 3: The Problem of Funding

The question that is surfacing more and more frequently is **how can we keep our jobs and volunteer programs from being reduced or dropped during funding cutbacks and downsizing?** What if we changed the question to **how will we become an employee and program that the organization will fight to keep?**

Most of you have read or heard what has become almost a mantra for our field. I first saw this saying on a poster at a friend's office and included it in my first book, *The Effective Management of Volunteer Programs*.

We, the willing,
led by the unknowing
are doing the impossible for the ungrateful.

We have done so much, for so long, with so little,
 we're qualified to anything with nothing.

It's often been quoted with a sort of "poor us" fashion as we discuss inadequate salaries and lack of support to do our work.

From our parasail viewpoint, let's look at it from a different perspective—one that acknowledges that we are in fact miracle workers and without a doubt the most creative entrepreneurs in the whole organization. Let's capitalize on just that fact as we sell the importance of our program and positions.

Of course, we also need to be smart enough to speak the rubric of the decision makers such as "bottom line," "return on investment," and "value added." In view of the threat of still more funding cuts, let's remind ourselves of the strengths we have!

The **bottom line/return on investment** is staggering when you consider that the accepted value of the volunteer hour is now $14.56 (1998).[9]

Value added is where we shine, for we are the link to government and corporate involvement. Keep these points in mind:

- Community volunteers are voters.
- Community volunteers are donors for volunteer agencies and give two-and-a-half times more than non-volunteers.
- Funders and foundations are looking carefully and seriously at the quality of volunteer programs as they consider funding requests for agencies.

Now I ask you, who in their right mind would knowingly fire a miracle worker today?

Issue 4: Risk Management

A question currently being asked by organizations is **"How can we keep from being sued?"** It has had a chilling and sometimes immobilizing effect on many volunteer programs because the obvious answer is to become more and more restrictive regarding the activities of volunteers, which in turn limits agency exposure.

Again, I would suggest the question itself is wrong. It should be **"How can we provide a safe environment for our clients, volunteers and staff in the process of achieving our mission"?** This suggests the need for developing sound and sensible risk management practices and policies that are both necessary and appropriate (background checks on all volunteers working with vulnerable client populations). An organization that has provided invaluable guidance is the Non-Profit Risk Management Center in Washington D.C. (www.nonprofitrisk.org).

Issue 5: Your Role as Leader

Perhaps the question I hear most frequently from directors of volunteers and trainers in our field is: **How can I keep from burning out?**

It's obvious many of us don't find the answer to this one since our turn-over time in this field is generally 3-5 years. The truth of the matter is that this has a devastating effect, not only on the directors and their volunteers programs, but on our field as a profession as well. People rarely stay around long enough to develop into leaders. So, do we just wring our hands and say that's just the way it is today or are there things we can do to alleviate it? May I share a few suggestions? These coming from a slow learner who's come very close to burnout—three times!

Now, let's again change the question from, "How do I avoid burnout?" to **"How can I stay well and creative as a leader in today's bullet train society?"** The first step is to shift the emphasis from roles to relationships.

I learned a profound lesson about this during the past few months. For over a month, I had the incredible privilege of being parented by my children and for the past several months I have shed the role of "giver" and have learned to be a grateful and gracious "receiver." What a deepening of relationships this shedding of roles has created.

The goal of developing relationships and shedding roles is critical, not just for our personal well-being but for our ability to be future leaders as well. Margaret Wheatley, in her book, *Leadership and the New Science,*[10] talks about the need to let go of our present models of work and refocus on the deep longings we have for community, meaning, dignity and love in our organizational lives. To do that, we'll need to become savvy about building relationships and how to nurture growing, evolving things. This requires better skills in listening, communication and facilitating groups, because these are the talents that build strong relationships. Relationships instead of roles or tasks, functions and hierarchies are the cornerstone of the new organization in a quantum world.

When you've confronted those unrealistic role expectations (many self-inflicted) you can then begin the second major step to staying well, discovering and developing that unique, one-of-a-kind, wonderful person called you. As one sage put it, "be yourself – no one else is better qualified." To help you do that, let's ponder a Native American concept I once heard:

> *Everyone is a house with four rooms—a physical, a mental, an emotional and a spiritual. Most of us tend to live in one room most of the time, but unless we go into every room every day, even if only to keep it aired, we are not a complete person.*

What a vivid metaphor for health and wholeness! If we're serious about staying well, we'll find time to:

- Do the necessary housecleaning to rid our rooms of clutter and toxic waste. It means "letting go" of lots of stuff! Never stumble on anything behind you.
- Know your own needs and be able and willing to articulate them clearly and honestly.

Another thing about your personal house is to be sure to not only visit each of the rooms everyday, but slowly and lovingly furnish those rooms with things that nourish and replenish you and give you joy. No one can do that for you. As Thomas Moore advises in *Care of the Soul*, "We need to be the artists and poets of our own lives."[11]

It's when we get our personal house in order that we are more able to be creative. And, when we are more creative we are open to all three types of creative insights:

- **The AHs:** Having keen sensory perception of the beauty and metaphors that surround us. We see them and experience the WOW reaction.
- **The HA-HAs:** The comic insights that occur when we laugh together. Laughter is one of the traits of exceptionally creative groups.
- **The A-HAs:** Those startling, most often fleeting insights we all get that cause an almost physical reaction, like an electric shock. Those mean you've just had your own personal creative revelation. They're precious and powerful! I hope you've had some during these past few days, in workshops, during keynote speeches or in late night conversations with colleagues. My advice to you is to carry an A-HA pad with you and especially have one by your bedside. It's the A-HAs that change the world.[12]

What do you do with creative insights when you go home? Let me share two experiences that were invaluable for me regarding my own creativity:

The first was a bit of wisdom from an 85-year-old friend, one of the first volunteers at the Volunteer and Information Center I helped create thirty years ago. I asked Clara's advice regarding taking on a major challenge. She said, "Say 'yes' to the big Marlene, or your life will fill up with the little." Do you remember the book entitled, *Don't Sweat the Small Stuff: It's All Small Stuff*? I've thought about this and have come to disagree. It's not all small stuff; wisdom is knowing the difference. Another interesting thing I've learned about "A-ha" moments is they are usually very pertinent to the present and, if not acted on, the opportunity can easily become lost.

The second insight was to never make a decision regarding "A-ha" (or "big") dreams based on logistics. Say "yes" and then figure out how to make it happen—that's the fun and creative part. I've never known how to do anything I've accomplished in this field when I first decided to do it. That includes writing a book, becoming my own publisher, establishing a volunteer center, becoming a founder and faculty director for a volunteer certificate training program or producing videos.

What I have experienced over and over again is the incredible truth expressed by Joseph Campbell: "Follow your bliss and doors will open where there were no doors before...and you will experience a thousand unseen helping hands."[13]

A Vision for Volunteerism in the New Century

As I look toward the new century and the multiplicity of issues, challenges, difficulties and opportunities we've just discussed (and many we haven't) my personal goal is to remain an "optimistic pragmatist," informed and hopeful.

There is no crystal ball, and I have been around long enough to not even pretend to try to predict the future. Annie Dillard observed, "We are most deeply asleep at the switch when we fancy we control any switches at all."[14] Or, as Woody Allen put it, "If you want to make God laugh, just tell him what your future plans are."

I saw an interview on the *CBS Sunday Morning Show* on February 8, 1998. The guest was the talented Maestro Seiji Ozawa who conducted the chorus and orchestra in an amazing rendition of *Ode to Joy* during the Opening Ceremonies at the Winter Olympics in Nagano, Japan. He conducted five choirs and five orchestras simultaneously from five continents connected by satellite. As the marvelous music filled the stadium and airways from Beijing, Sydney, Cape Town, Berlin and the United States it was impossible not to weep, it was so magnificent.

In the interview, Ozawa said he "wanted the music to come from all the people...all for joy...everybody, everywhere at the same time...then it becomes a prayer." He grew up in the mountains outside of Nagano and he even recruited some of those mountain people to come to the stadium and join in the choir. He wasn't worried that they didn't know how to sing, he just said, "We teach them."

In responding to a compliment about the beauty of his music, Ozawa said humbly, "I don't make music, the orchestra makes the music. All I can do is invite them to make sound." This, my friends, is perhaps the best definition of a volunteer manager I've ever heard.

And, what a magnificent vision for the future of volunteerism:

- Using the wonders of technology and the blurring of global boundaries to lead the efforts of volunteers around the globe—combining not just their voices, but their energy, talents and creativity to truly make the world a better place for all of us. What fun it would be to have an International "Make a Difference Day" beamed by satellite around the world during the International Year of Volunteers 2001.

- To be leaders who are wise enough to know that we don't make the music, we invite the volunteers to make their own music. And we are the teachers and mentors to help those who don't yet know how, so they can join us.

Let's adopt *Ode to Joy* as our theme song.

[1] Stanley Davies and Christopher Meyer, *Blur: The Speed of Change in the Connected Economy* (New York: Warner Books, 1998).

[2] Sara Ban Breathnach, *Simple Abundance* (Grand Central Publishing, 1995).

[3] Susan J. Ellis and Katherine Noyes, *By the People: A History of Americans as Volunteers* (Jossey-Bass, 1990), 4.

[4] Sarah Jane Rehnborg, "The Limits of the 'V' Word: Communicating What We Really Do," *Energize, Inc. Hot Topic*, (October 1998), http://www.energizeinc.com/hot/oct98.html (accessed April 2008).

[5] At the time of publishing this book, Betty Stallings sells her *55-Minute Training Series* as downloadable PDF files.

[6] The University of Colorado Volunteer Management Certificate Program ended in 1997. Contact your local volunteer center for copies of the courses on video.

[7] Will Rogers, *Will Rogers Wise and Witty Sayings* (Castle Press, 1969).

[8] http://www.serviceleader.org/new/virtual/ (accessed April 2008).

[9] At the time of publishing this book, the value of the volunteer hour was reported by the Independent Sector to be $19.51 for 2007. http://www.independentsector.org/programs/research/volunteer_time.html (accessed April 2008).

[10] Margaret Wheatley, *Leadership and The New Science: Learning about Organization from an Orderly Universe* (Berrett-Koehler Publishers, 1984).

[11] Thomas Moore, *Care of the Soul* (HarperPerennial, 1992).

[12] Adapted from a speech by William J. Bersely, "From Ha-Has to A-has to Ahs: The Wisdom of Wit" http://www.callutheran.edu/news/speakers/speaker_detail.php?profile_id=9 (accessed April 2008).

[13] Joseph Campbell, *The Power of Myth* (Doubleday, 1988), 120.

[14] Annie Dillard, *Holy the Firm* (Harper Collins, 1977), 62.

Section III:
Epilogue: The Why Behind Everything

A Philosophy of Volunteerism
(What I Thought at the Beginning of My Career)

※

Volunteer and Information Center Annual Meeting
Boulder, CO, May 1977

Comments: *This speech was given at the 8th annual meeting of the Boulder County Volunteer and Information Center (VIC) in May 1977 as I was about to leave the Center and begin giving workshops and conferences through the United States and Canada. I was one of the founders and first executive director of VIC and it is where I learned almost everything I know and believe about volunteers and volunteer management. What I've written and taught for 35 years has been taken from the bed-rock foundation of my seven years directing VIC.*

I want to thank all of you for many things, and they are things that are difficult to put into words—but I'll try. First, I am grateful that it was during my VIC adventure that I came to understand and experience first-hand what the pioneering social scientist, Eduard Lindeman, said about volunteers long ago: "I wish I knew how to induce volunteers to appreciate the significant role they play in offering vitality to the democratic enterprise. They are to democracy what circulation of blood is to the organism, they keep democracy alive!"

And, I might add, you keep VIC alive! This may sound like just another platitude, but believing it and passing on that belief has become a whole way of life for me. It is the *why* behind my books and my workshops.

Because I know from experience the joy and excitement of working creatively with a volunteer team, my heart aches to know that today the #1 problem in volunteer programs nationally is volunteer/staff relationships. It's tragic! So, it's important for you to know you're being used nationally as an example of the fact that it can and does work.

This partnership as we experienced it, and I hope I speak for those of you who were involved with me in it, both volunteer and paid, can be described in the words of Elizabeth O'Connor in *Search for Silence*:

> *The experience of centered lives can be one of creativity, of a pervading presence, of joy, of quiet contagious excitement, differing from time to time, but always issuing in community. One has the feeling of being in on what is important and wanting others to be in on it also.*[1]

Now this in no way means I've become Pollyanna-ish and do not recognize or admit that the experience had some pain sprinkled liberally in with the joy. Being involved at VIC has been an experience not without joy or without pain for every single one of us in this room. That's what has made it authentic, for that's how life is. But today, I want to focus on the joy.

The second thing I'm grateful for today is the opportunity VIC gave me and others to grow...to become, as persons. I feel blessed to have stumbled (or was it being led?) to that small band of dreamers that had the vision that became VIC. I had no knowledge of volunteers at that time, except the usual "helping out" as neighbor, parent, or churchwoman. I had no idea there was a "field of volunteerism" at all. I simply remember my intent was to volunteer 30 hours a week of my time for three months to help Ivan and the committee get it organized. That was 8 ½ years ago.

If I had known where it all was going to lead, I would probably have been so scared I would have opted for golf or belly dance classes or stuck to watching *The Edge of Night*. At least those were predictable. But thank God it didn't happen, for it has been 8 ½ years of discovery of myself and others. This journey of becoming has illustrated what John Gardner meant when he talked about exploring our potentialities. He said it goes beyond just skills to the full range of our capacities for sensing, wondering, learning, understanding, loving and aspiring.

The great thing about working in human services today is that this journey need never end. We are constantly faced with the need to grow, adapt and respond to new realities. Volunteerism today is like a giant puzzle whose pieces are amoebic—they keep changing shapes all the time. It's hard to ever get it all put together and have it stay put. It seems like just as we learn the right answers, someone changes the questions and we have to start again.

Perhaps it would be reassuring to know it's not just VIC and RSVP (Retired Senior Volunteer Program, a program started by VIC), but the human service world in general. Some things we're observing:

- Agencies' services and priorities change, often due to funding shifts
- Community needs are changing (economic, environmental)
- The volunteer work force is undergoing tremendous change:
  - More men
  - More working people
  - More students and seniors
  - Fewer women of ages 25-45
- More clients
- Government priorities change
- More competition for the volunteer
- More serious consideration of what is required to run effective programs in constantly changing realities

I learned a standard farewell in a Mexican village is "May you go with God and may nothing new happen to you."

Marlene, 1977

Since the only constant we seem to have is change, perhaps what we need to do is begin to educate ourselves accordingly and not just hope it goes away. John Gardener identified two ways to educate:

- We can indoctrinate people in an elaborate set of fixed beliefs (which ensures their early obsolescence) or
- Help develop skills, attitudes, habits of mind and the kinds of knowledge and understanding that will help a person continuously grow and change. A system that provides for its own continuous renewal. Society decays when its institutions and individuals lose their vitality. The last act of a dying institution is to put out a new, enlarged rulebook.[2]

The second choice is educating for innovation, creativity and versatility. This kind of education helps people cope with unforeseen challenges and survive as versatile individuals in an unpredictable world. There is danger in this kind of education though. Rollo May says these people become "forever unsatisfied with the mundane, the apathetic, the conventional. They always push on to newer worlds."[3] And, I might add, the world almost always pushes back.

Perhaps the very essence of my VIC experience was that I found myself surrounded by just these kinds of people and the effect on me was exhilarating and profound. The secret of success for VIC and RSVP was, and I'm sure still is, the coming together of people who see things as they might be and say, "why not?" And, in the process, each person's own journey of becoming is consciously welcomed and enabled. This journey is exciting, demanding, joyous and frustrating.

In closing, I'd like to share this quotation from Martin Bell's *The Way of the Wolf*.

> *I think God must be very old and very tired. Maybe he used to look splendid and fine in his general's uniform but no more. He's been on the march a long time, you know. And look at his rag-tag little army! All he has for soldiers are you and me. Dumb little army. Listen! The drumbeat isn't even regular. Everyone is out of step. And there! You see? God keeps stopping along the way to pick up one of his tiniest soldiers who decided to wander off and play with a frog, or run in a field, or whose foot got tangled in the underbrush. He'll never get anywhere that way. And yet, the march goes on.*

> *Do you see how the marchers have broken up into little groups? Look at that group up near the front. Now, there's a snappy outfit. They all look pretty much alike, at least they're in step with each other. That's something! Only they're not wearing their shoes. They're carrying them in their hands. Silly little band. They won't get far before God will have to stop again.*

Or how about that other group over there? They're all holding hands as they march. The only trouble with this is the men on each end of the line. Pretty soon they realize that one of their hands isn't holding onto anything – one hand is reaching, empty, alone. And so around in circles. The more people holding hands, the bigger the circle. And of course, a bigger circle is deceptive because as we march along it looks like we're going someplace, which we're not. And so God must stop again, you see what I mean? He'll never get anywhere that way!

If God were sensible he'd take his little army and shape them up. Why, whoever heard of a soldier stopping to romp in a field? It's ridiculous, but even more absurd is a general who will stop the march of eternity to go and bring him back. But that's God for you. His is no endless, empty marching. He is going somewhere. His steps are deliberate and purposeful. He may be old, and he may be tired. But he knows where he's going. And he means to take every last one of his tiny soldiers with him. Only there are frogs and flowers and thorns and underbrush. And most of us are afraid and lonely and would like to hold hands or cry or run away. And we don't know where we are going, and we can't seem to trust God—especially when it's dark out and we can't see him! And he won't go on without us. And that's why it's taking so long.

Listen! The drum beat isn't even regular. Everyone is out of step. And there! You see? God keeps stopping along the way to pick up one of his tiniest soldiers who decided to wander off and play with a frog, or run in a field, or whose foot got tangled in the underbrush. He'll never get anywhere that way!

And yet, the march goes on.... [4]

[1] Elizabeth O'Connor, *Search for Silence* (Word Books, 1974), 94.

[2] John Gardener, *On Leadership*, (The Free Press, 1990), 157.

[3] Rollo May, *The Courage to Create* (W.W. Norton & Co. 1975), 32.

[4] Martin Bell, *The Way of the Wolf: The Gospel in New Images* (Seabury Press, 1970).

What I Still Believe

Spring 2008

Many of the people who urged me to write this book said they really hoped I would share some wisdom, insights and inspiration from my vantage point of age and experience.

This request got me thinking about the concept of wisdom—and led me to revisit one of my favorite quotes of T.S. Elliott:

Where is the life we have lost in living?
Where is the wisdom we have lost in knowledge?
Where is the knowledge we have lost in information?[1]

So—as I pondered the idea of wisdom, and reflected on this quote, I decided these are the things I believe about wisdom.

- Wisdom deals with the *why* questions; knowledge and information deal with the *what* and *how*.
- Wisdom deals with future implications; knowledge and information tend to concentrate on the present.
- Wisdom deals with principles and values (paradigms); knowledge and information deal with practices.
- Wisdom seeks to understand the questions; knowledge and information look for the answers.
- Wisdom is going deeper; knowledge and information tend to just keep getting broader.

In summary, wisdom deals with the *whys* of what we do; with the future implications of our decisions; with the principles and values underlying our decisions and practices; with being willing to ask the hard questions; and to keep going deeper into the meaning of our profession.

I am in no way implying that knowledge and information are not important. They are essential to help us reshape, re-form and innovate our practices in this field. Knowledge and information keep us viable and appropriate in dealing with all the trends. T.S. Elliott also wrote: "We shall not cease from exploration and the end of all exploring will be to arrive where we started—and know the place for the first time."[2]

So, in my exploring I began to ask, what do I still believe about leadership and management and volunteerism and groups that have stood the test of time...actually almost 40 years of writing, teaching and doing volunteer management? And, I realize that what I've held fast to is a number of powerful principles that were there for me when I started—but now I know them in a new way from the vantage point of age and experience. At the same time, the knowledge, information and application of these principles have changed dramatically over the years. In other words, my *whys* have stayed the same—but the *whats* and *hows* have needed to change with the tides and trends of change. I honestly think this is what has provided my "staying power" all these years.

Let me share a few of these powerful principles with you—knowing the real value will be to encourage you to make your own list.

My Powerful Principles (What I Still Believe)

Volunteers are not paid – not because they're worthless, but because they're priceless!

I heard this quote over 30 years ago. It reflects the strong belief I have about volunteers and it has been my guiding principle in all the work I've done in developing systems and practices to work effectively and caringly with them.

Contrast this attitude towards volunteers we've all witnessed:

"Volunteers are nice, but not necessary."

"Volunteers are more work than they're worth."

"They're OK, as long as they don't cost us anything."

"We'll use them to save money, but they should be seen and not heard."

The attitudes of your key people towards volunteers permeate your organization and have a dramatic effect on the climate (how volunteers feel about working).

People must be as important as programs, products or profits.

The truth is that leaders either grow or diminish those who work with them. Therefore, if we meet our goals at the expense of the health and well-being and growth of our people—we have ultimately failed.

Marlene, 2008

Marlene, 2008

Examples:
- In the 1950s, programs became the focus of churches and people started leaving.
- In the 1990s and 2000s, corporations focused so much on products and profits, they killed their own people. They abandoned principles and emphasized *what, how,* and *what's in it for me.* The *whys* and the values got lost.

People become committed to plans they help make; so plan *with*, not *for* people.

This idea has gone through several fads and phases the past few years—like participative management and quality circles. Organizations spent millions bringing in gurus to teach them *how* but many of these efforts ultimately failed because the leaders didn't understand the *why*, which was Margaret Mead's profound observation, "The wisdom is in the group!"

Far too often, it became a gimmick to manipulate a group—and it failed. People are too smart for this! Stephen Covey observed, "It simply makes no difference how good the rhetoric is or even how good the intentions are; if there is little or no trust, there is no foundation for permanent success. Only basic goodness gives life to techniques."[3]

Mission motivates – maintenance does not.

That's why one of the leader's primary tasks is casting the vision, and keeping it alive!

A vision without a task is but a dream.
A task without a vision is drudgery.
A vision and a task is the hope of the world.
—From a church in England, 1730

Make sure everyone who works with you, volunteers and staff, knows your mission and how their work makes it happen.

Integrity is the leader's most powerful asset.

And it has to be carefully and patiently *earned*. The foundation for all team building should be three pronged:
- Truth
- Trust
- Clear expectations

Avoid the trap of becoming either a specialist or a generalist.

A *specialist* is someone who knows more and more about less and less, until they know practically everything about almost nothing.

A *generalist* is someone who knows less and less about more and more until they know almost nothing about everything.

Be yourself—no one else is better qualified.

In other words, be true to your principles and not swayed by fad or fashion.

There is no substitute for being congruent in what you say and what you do—it builds trust in others and gives you peace of mind. For example, it is essential you work with volunteers yourselves. It's what gives you credibility and makes you an effective advocate for volunteerism.

The key to wise leadership is effective delegation and the key to delegation (and motivation) is getting the right people in the right jobs.

May I share a tip with you that has served me well for many years? Do not only *accept* but actually *seek out* someone who knows more than you do where you need help; then let them do it and be glad they succeed!

How do you get the right people in the right jobs? Know them by talking to them (interviewing) and observing them in action. Watch when their eyes light up! McClelland's Theory of Motivation of achievers, affiliators, and power people has been incredibly helpful to me. It's described in detail previously in this book in the presentation called "Motivation: Placing Right People in Right Jobs."

Motivation of others is critical to your success.

I believe what John Gardner said about motivation:

Leaders don't create motivation they unlock it. They must be on the side of hopefulness and instill in their people that they can have an impact. They have to help people find the things that are worth committing to...it is the leader's job to keep the dreams alive![4]

Let your own enthusiasm, excitement and dedication to your mission shine through your work—it's contagious! My husband, Harvey, used to say to me, "You love what you do so much you don't even know it's work!" How blessed I've been.

To become advocates and innovators, develop the 3 Cs:
- Curiosity
- Creativity
- Courage

Be alert to those problems and challenges that "have your name on them" (due to your past experience and skill) and take ownership of them.

Don't worry about knowing *how* to solve the problem, figuring it out is the fun part. And remember, you don't need to know how it will all come out. There is a wonderful flow of past, present, and future. The wisdom of knowing *when* to let go is so important and difficult. But equally important is to know when to step up to the plate and take on issues.

I can't help others if I don't stay well myself. So take care of me!

Maya Angelo once said, "to survive is important – to thrive with passion, compassion and style is elegant." That's my goal.

As I quoted previously, I admire the Native American concept that states:

Everyone is a house with four rooms – a physical, a mental, an emotional and a spiritual. Most of us tend to live in one room most of the time. But unless we

go into every room every day, even if only to keep it aired, we are not a complete
person.

What a vivid metaphor for health and wholeness! I still firmly believe if
we're serious about staying well, we'll *find* time to:

- Do the necessary housecleaning to rid our rooms of clutter and toxic
  waste – "letting go" of lots of stuff!
- Know your own needs. If you can't name your own needs you don't
  deserve to have them met.
- Be sure we not only visit each room every day, but slowly and
  lovingly furnish those rooms with things that nourish and replenish
  us and give us joy.

No one can do that for you. As Thomas Moore advises in *Care of the Soul,* "We
need to be the artists and poets of our own lives."[5]

It is important to keep the soul in our work.

It is said about Louie Armstrong that there were no barriers between his
soul and his horn.

Wayne Muller tells the story of a South American tribe that would go on
long marches, day after day. All of a sudden, they would stop walking, sit
down, rest and then make camp for a couple of days. They explained that they
needed the time to rest *so that their souls could catch up with them.* A wonderful
concept.

In closing, my hope for all of you is that you will rise to these new challenges
with clear vision, a list of your own powerful principles, new creative how-
tos and all the energy, enthusiasm, dedication, joy…and yes, soul, you have!
That you have the wisdom to determine what to keep, what to change, what
to drop and what to create. *You* are the future of volunteerism.

To do this you need the courage of pioneers, the ingenuity of entrepreneurs,
the enthusiasm and the fearlessness of 5-year-olds, the dedication and
compassion of volunteers and the wisdom of Solomon.

Oh yes…and I almost forgot the faith that nothing worthwhile is ever
impossible!

[1] T.S. Eliot, Choruses from "The Rock," *The Complete Poems and Plays* (Harcourt, Brace
and Co., 1952), 96.

[2] T.S. Eliot, "Little Gidding," *Four Quartets* (Harcourt, Brace and Co., 1943).

[3] Stephen Covey, *The Seven Habits of Highly Effective People* (Free Press, 1989), 21.

[4] John Gardener, *On Leadership* (Free Press, 1990), 14.

[5] Thomas Moore, *Care of the Soul* (HarperPerennial, 1992), 300.

Closing Thoughts

Susan J. Ellis

Energize, Inc. is thrilled to offer this record of Marlene Wilson's presentations to two audiences: those of you who were lucky enough to have heard Marlene give one or more of these speeches, and those of you who have met her for the first time in these pages. For the former, we hope Marlene's words re-inspire you, just as you felt when you heard them live. By capturing Marlene's vision in this book, we want to keep reaching an ever-growing number of "first timers," in the hope that you will build a strong future on her legacy.

As you learned in Marlene's presentation "Our Profession at a Crossroads," I first met Marlene as a very young practitioner and have been privileged to know her for over 30 years. She led the way for all the other authors, consultants and trainers. She was one of the first to go on the road to train volunteer program managers and put a professional face on the work we do. Her first book, *The Effective Management of Volunteer Programs*, arrived in 1976 and stood alone for over a decade as the only comprehensive guide to the principles of engaging volunteers in agencies. Everyone owned it and read it more than once.

As it happened, Marlene advised Katie Campbell (at that time, Katie Noyes) and me about how to publish the first edition of our book, *By the People: A History of Americans as Volunteers*. In 1978 it became the third title in the field. So it feels like coming full-circle for Energize to be the publisher today of this career-long compilation by Marlene.

Some may not know that Marlene was a pioneer in identifying churches and the rest of the faith community as the "sleeping giant" of volunteerism (a title of one of her articles long ago). Her 1983 book, *How to Mobilize Church Volunteers*, became another bible (excuse the pun) for directors of lay ministry everywhere. She continues to pursue a lifelong mission to strengthen how congregations work together, both to serve one another and to address social concerns.

The earliest presentation in this book was delivered 1974 and the most recent in 1999. Here and there you'll find a reference to things in society that have changed, yet Marlene's essential messages are not dated. There's continuity throughout her recommendations and exhortations, especially when it comes to urging our profession to look ahead. Along with finding motivational quotes from people way beyond our own field, she often used demographic statistics, economic change data, and other information on measurable trends in her speeches. Marlene always attempted to make volunteer program leaders aware of the interplay between current news headlines and what would soon affect the availability and interests of volunteers. Her premise continues to be critical as the pace of change increases.

Unfortunately, the profession of volunteer administration in the United States in presently facing serious challenges. You'll see that many of the presentations in this book occurred during what eventually was called the International Conference on Volunteer Administration (ICVA), considered by most to be the best annual conference in our field. It was sponsored by the professional society that we knew as AVA—the Association for Volunteer Administration. With startling and dismaying speed, AVA ceased to operate in 2006 and, with its demise, the ICVA ended as well. As of 2008, as this book appears, there is still a significant vacuum for those of us in the United States: no clear successor to AVA and no national conference targeted specifically to leaders of volunteer efforts. This state of affairs would have been inconceivable to most of us even a few years ago. So Marlene's vision of our professional future needs to be taken very seriously…and fought for.

Despite serious concerns in the U.S. about the infrastructure of volunteerism here, the wonderful news is that the rest of the world is stepping up to the plate. In the two years since AVA ended, brand new or revitalized professional societies have launched in England and Singapore. The Australasian Association of Volunteer Administrators (AAVA) is growing in numbers. The first-ever Asia Pacific Conference for Volunteer Leadership will be held in Hawaii in September 2008. The European Volunteer Centre (CEV) is a network of 60 mainly national and regional volunteer development agencies across Europe, working "to support and promote voluntary activity." The International Association for Volunteer Effort (IAVE) continues to convene several thousand participants at its biannual international conference, the 2008 event held in Panama. And this brief synopsis of progress only scratches the surface.

So, we offer Marlene's book for inspiration and vision, in the hope that it will motivate readers to revitalize—or grow—our field anywhere volunteers need great leadership. Which, of course, is everywhere.

1931471

Made in the USA